D1709015

Working with Data

Facilitator's Guide

A collaborative project by the staff and
participants of Teaching to the Big Ideas

Principal Investigators

Susan Jo Russell
Deborah Schifter
Virginia Bastable

with
Traci L. Higgins
Jill Bodner Lester

DALE SEYMOUR PUBLICATIONS
Pearson Learning Group

 **National Science Foundation**

ExxonMobil

This work was supported by the National Science Foundation under Grant Nos. ESI-9254393 and ESI-9731064. Any opinions, findings, conclusions, or recommendations expressed here are those of the authors and do not necessarily reflect the views of the National Science Foundation.

Additional support was provided by a grant from the ExxonMobil Foundation.

Art & Design: Jim O'Shea, Elizabeth Nemeth

Editorial: Beverly Cory, Doris Hirschhorn

Manufacturing: Mark Cirillo, Sonia Pap

Marketing: Margo Hanson

Production: Karen Edmonds, Jennifer Murphy

Publishing Operations: Carolyn Coyle

ISBN 0-7690-2792-X
Printed in the United States of America
2 3 4 5 6 7 8 9 10 11   07 06 05 04 03

 **Dale Seymour Publications**
Pearson Learning Group

1-800-321-3106
www.pearsonlearning.com

Teaching to the Big Ideas

Developing Mathematical Ideas (DMI) was developed as a collaborative project by the staff and participants of Teaching to the Big Ideas, an NSF Teacher Enhancement Project.

PROJECT DIRECTORS   Deborah Schifter (EDC), Virginia Bastable (SummerMath for Teachers), Susan Jo Russell (TERC)

STAFF   Traci L. Higgins (TERC), Jill Bodner Lester (SummerMath for Teachers)

PARTICIPANTS   Marie Appleby, Allan Arnaboldi, Lisa Bailly, Audrey Barzey, Katie Bloomfield, Nancy Buell, Rose Christiansen, Rebeka Eston, Kimberly Formisano, Connie Henry, Nancy Horowitz, Debbie Jacque, Liliana Klass, Beth Monopoli, Deborah Morrissey, Amy Morse, Deborah Carey O'Brien, Karin Olson, Anne Marie O'Reilly, Janet Pananos, Margie Riddle, Bette Ann Rodzwell, Jan Rook, Karen Schweitzer, Malia Scott, Lisa Seyferth, Margie Singer, Susan Bush Smith, Diane Stafford, Michele Subocz, Liz Sweeney, Pam Szczesny, Jan Szymaszek, Nora Toney, Polly Wagner, and Carol Walker, representing the public schools of Amherst, Boston, Brookline, Lexington, Lincoln, Newton, Northampton, Pelham, Shutesbury, South Hadley, Southampton, Springfield, and Williamsburg, Massachusetts; the Atrium School in Watertown, Massachusetts; the Park School in Brookline, Massachusetts; the Smith College Campus School in Northampton, Massachusetts

VIDEO DEVELOPMENT   David Smith (TERC)

CONSULTANTS, *WORKING WITH DATA*   Mike Battista (Kent State University), Herb Clemens (University of Utah), Doug Clements (State University of New York at Buffalo), Clifford Konold (University of Massachusetts at Amherst), Rich Lehrer (University of Wisconsin), Steve Monk (University of Washington), Judy Roitman (University of Kansas), Richard Scheaffer (University of Florida)

FIELD TEST SITES   Albuquerque Public Schools (New Mexico); Durham Public Schools (North Carolina); Lake Washington School District (Washington); Milwaukee Public Schools (Wisconsin); Northampton Public Schools (Massachusetts); University of Illinois, Chicago

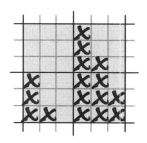

C O N T E N T S

Maxine's Journal (continued)

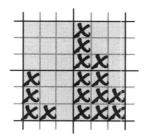

Orientation to the Materials

Developing Mathematical Ideas (DMI) is a professional development curriculum designed to help teachers think through the major ideas of K–7 mathematics and examine how children develop those ideas. At the heart of the DMI materials are the casebooks filled with classroom episodes that illustrate students' mathematical thinking as described by their teachers. In addition to reading and discussing these cases, participants in a DMI seminar explore mathematics in lessons led by facilitators, share and discuss the work of their own students, view and discuss videotapes of mathematics classrooms, write up episodes from their own classrooms, analyze lessons from innovative elementary mathematics curricula, and read overviews of related research.

DMI seminars bring together teachers from kindergarten through the middle grades and help these teachers

- learn mathematics content

- recognize key mathematical ideas with which their students are grappling

- find ways to support the power and complexity of student thinking

- discover how core mathematical ideas develop across the grades

- learn how to *continue* learning about children and mathematics

School systems that have adopted innovative mathematics curricula have found DMI to be an important support. The materials have been used with practicing teachers in both summer institutes and school-year settings. In addition, DMI has served as core curriculum for programs designed for teacher-leaders, administrators, parents, and pre-service teachers.

The DMI curriculum is presented through a series of five seminars, each focusing on a different content area of mathematics.

Number and Operations, Part 1: Building a System of Tens

Participants explore the base ten structure of the number system; they consider how that structure is used in multidigit computational procedures; and they learn how the basic concepts of whole numbers reappear in work with decimals.

Number and Operations, Part 2: Making Meaning for Operations

Participants examine the actions and situations modeled by the four basic operations. The seminar begins with a view of young children's counting strategies as they encounter word problems, moves to an examination of the four basic operations on whole numbers, and revisits the operations in the context of rational numbers.

Geometry: Examining Features of Shape

Participants examine aspects of two- and three-dimensional shapes, develop geometric vocabulary, and explore both definitions and properties of geometric objects. The seminar includes a study of angle, similarity, congruence, and the relationships between 3-D objects and their 2-D representations.

Geometry: Measuring Space in One, Two, and Three Dimensions

Participants examine different aspects of size, develop facility in composing and decomposing shapes, and apply these skills to make sense of formulas for area and volume. They also explore conceptual issues of length, area, and volume, as well as the complex interrelationships among these.

Statistics: Working with Data

Participants work with the collection, representation, description, and interpretation of data. They learn what various types of graphs and statistical measures show about features of the data; they learn how to summarize data in order to compare groups; and they consider whether the data provide insight into the questions that initially led to data collection.

Materials for participants

Casebook   Each seminar is built around a casebook containing 25 to 35 cases, grouped into seven chapters, which track a set of mathematical ideas from kindergarten into the middle grades. Casebooks begin with an introduction to the seminar, and each chapter starts with an overview that orients the reader to the major theme of the cases in that chapter. Each casebook concludes with an essay entitled "Highlights of Related Research." After working through seven sets of cases to explore children's mathematical thinking through the eyes of teachers working in classroom contexts, seminar participants now consider these same issues from a research perspective. Each of these essays presents research findings in jargon-free, accessible language.

Materials for facilitators

Facilitator's guides   These provide detailed agendas for each session. In addition, a large portion of each guide is "Maxine's Journal," the writings of a fictional facilitator describing the events and individuals encountered in one seminar, including her responses to their thinking and their written work. Together, the two sections of the guide help facilitators identify particular strategies useful in leading case discussions and mathematics activities, plan seminar sessions, understand the major ideas to be explored in each session, and think through issues of teacher change.

Video cases   While written cases allow users to examine student thinking at their own pace and to return as needed to ponder and analyze particular passages, the video offers users the opportunity to listen to real student voices in real time and provides rich images of classrooms organized around student thinking. The video cases show a wide variety of classroom settings, with children and teachers of different ethnic and language groups.

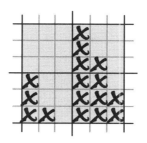

Tips for Facilitators

The DMI curriculum was piloted in a range of settings by facilitators with varying professional backgrounds. These facilitators included university faculty, staff development personnel, and teachers working with colleagues. For some, leading a DMI seminar was their first experience as a teacher-leader or teacher educator; others had many years of service in this role.

Through conversations and written reflections, the seminar facilitators provided valuable feedback about their experiences piloting this curriculum. The following tips include their suggestions, some directly quoted, for getting oriented to the materials, preparing for individual seminar sessions, creating a community of inquiry, facilitating discussion, understanding participants' emotions, responding to the written portfolio assignments, and adjusting the curriculum to different formats and constituencies. This section concludes with an annotated bibliography of recommended supplemental readings for seminar participants and facilitators.

Getting oriented

Before conducting a DMI seminar, familiarize yourself with both the overall goals of the curriculum and the materials. You will be using these materials to support teachers as they (1) recognize themselves and the children they teach as mathematical thinkers, (2) deepen their understanding of the core ideas in the elementary mathematics curriculum, (3) explore how children develop those ideas, (4) reflect on their own experiences to analyze the process of learning, and (5) rethink their teaching practice.

As the facilitator, you will lead your group in the following types of activities:

- **Case discussions** In these discussions of the casebook, teachers strive to follow student thinking, work on mathematical ideas for themselves, reflect on their own learning, and consider the types of classroom settings and teaching strategies that support the development of student understanding.

- **Viewing the video cases** On the videotapes, teachers see episodes that capture both classroom atmosphere and student affect. These tapes give participants glimpses of children's mathematical thinking in process.

- **Mathematics activities** Through activities similar to those faced by students in the print and video cases, the teachers develop, share, analyze, and refine their own mathematical thinking.

- **Innovative curricular materials** By studying selected activities from existing mathematics curricula, teachers work to connect their seminar learning with the mathematical tasks they set for their students.

- **Discussing related research** This discussion toward the end of each seminar creates an integrated picture of the mathematical themes under consideration, connecting the events observed in the cases and in participants' own classrooms to the findings of the research community.

In addition, teachers complete regular written "portfolio assignments" between sessions, sometimes reflecting on what they are learning in the seminar, at other times taking a closer look into their own students' mathematical thinking.

To become familiar with the flow of mathematical ideas in the curriculum, we suggest that a facilitator read the introduction to the casebook, the overviews of the cases in each chapter, and the concluding essay on related research. We also recommend reading at least one session from "Maxine's Journal" to get a feel for the seminar experience. In addition, you may find it useful to examine some of the cases and look through the detailed agendas and handouts.

Preparing for a session

Once you are familiar with the goals and components of the DMI curriculum, the next step is to prepare for individual sessions. For each session, you should read the cases first, then the related entry of "Maxine's Journal" and the suggested agenda. Finally, you should work through the activities in the session yourself; for example, do the math activity, view the video, or familiarize yourself with the

selected lessons from the innovative curricula. As you do this work, think through the issues raised by that set of activities. What ideas about mathematics, learning, and teaching should emerge as teachers participate in the investigations and discussions? How are these ideas illustrated in the cases? How might they arise in the other activities? What questions might you pose to call attention to these ideas? As one facilitator wrote:

> I realize now more than ever how important it is to be really prepared and to have thought through the issues, mathematical and otherwise, that might arise. Having a sense of the important points that you want people to be exploring and the direction in which you want them to be headed is crucial. However, it is important to realize that sometimes "the way there" might turn out to be different from the route you anticipated.

Besides planning for issues likely to arise during discussions, you must think through the order of the activities and set a timetable. Organize the materials so everything is ready for each session; having the readings, handouts, videotapes, video equipment, and manipulatives at hand before a session saves time and allows you to concentrate on seminar participants. Suggestions for time allotments and the order of activities are given in the session agendas, along with lists of the materials you will need for each session.

Creating a community of inquiry

One objective of the DMI seminars is to establish a "community of inquiry," a sense of shared purpose and norms of conduct that allow participants to focus on ideas, both their own and those of their colleagues. This is not accomplished in a single session, but develops slowly. As one facilitator wrote:

I believe this climate of inquiry is created through careful work and planning over time with caring facilitators and willing participants. It never just happens. It requires constant nurturing, sensitivity, and organization.

Each teacher brings to the seminar his or her own experiences and ideas from which the others—and you, too—can learn much. It is your job, as facilitator, to encourage every participant to put those experiences and ideas on the table.

The facilitator should set the tone of the seminar at the very first meeting by demonstrating that all ideas are valued and questioning is perceived as a sign of strength, not weakness. Listening to what is said, rather than for what one expects, is crucial to creating a community in which ideas are heard and respected. What is the participant saying? What are the ideas behind the words? How are his or her ideas related to those of the other participants? How are they different? One facilitator wrote:

The purpose of [our] work is not about getting other teachers to think the same way, but rather to encourage an environment in which participants value, reflect on, and question their own ideas and the perspectives of others.

Another wrote:

As facilitators, we must create a pathway for learning that is challenging but safe. We must listen carefully to the comments our new fellow-travelers will share, empathize with their frustrations, help them through times of vulnerability, and share in the pleasures of their new insights.

Communicating clarity of purpose at the start of the seminar is vital to setting the tone. For instance, by making it clear that sessions will begin and end on time, you convey a message of commitment. As another facilitator put it:

Careful, productive, and appropriate use of time is a courtesy to the participants which indicates that you are respectful of their decision to be there in the midst of their busy lives and tight schedules.

Other ground rules to be addressed at the first meeting relate to assignments and attendance. Unlike many college courses or staff workshops, the success of the DMI seminar depends on participant preparation. Written homework and thoughtful reaction to assigned readings provide a starting point for the work of the session. Participants may have other expectations, so this should be stated explicitly. Attending each meeting with completed assignments prepares teachers to participate in planned activities and discussions and is a sign of respect for other members of the group.

Not all participants will feel comfortable speaking up or offering their opinions in whole-group discussion. Their involvement with the ideas of the DMI seminar can take many forms. People may be listening carefully, following the discussion, reflecting on what they hear, and formulating opinions of their own without sharing their thoughts aloud. Over time, participants will need support in seeking their own levels of verbal engagement. Among the strategies that encourage participation are allowing enough "wait time" for people to formulate their ideas, asking for a paraphrase of an idea, or asking for agreement or disagreement on particular points. During whole-group discussion, facilitators should ask clarifying questions, call attention to connections between participants' ideas, and pose questions designed to move the discussion forward.

The third session of Statistics: *Working with Data* includes an activity designed to help participants set group norms for respectful interaction. These norms should be revisited periodically throughout the seminar. Participants need to feel safe, whether sharing hypotheses or feelings. Adults' beliefs have developed over many years, and transforming those beliefs is a complicated process. Group leaders must cultivate an environment of inquiry, in which everyone's thinking is taken seriously and challenging someone's ideas is viewed as a sign of respect.

Facilitating group discussion

For seminar participants, small-group discussion provides a more intimate, certainly less intimidating forum for sharing their perspectives than does discussion among the whole group. In the small group, participants can explore mathematical ideas for themselves and pose questions about teaching, about learning, and about student understanding—all of which may feel riskier in the larger group. Furthermore, in a group of 2 to 4 people, there is more time to air ideas than in a group of 15 to 30.

While participants are meeting in small groups, what is the facilitator's role? When should you begin to move among the groups? When should you ask a question, add a comment, or just be a silent observer?

After setting small groups to work, allow time for them to get into meaningful discussion without being distracted by the facilitator. Then, once such discussion is underway, listen in on each of the small groups to get an overview of participants' interests, questions, and concerns. Moving among and stopping by each of the groups also communicates interest in the ideas being discussed and reassures participants

that their discussions are useful and productive.

Sometimes, people in small groups are "off task." It may then be necessary for the facilitator to focus the discussion on a specific point: evidence of mathematics learning presented in the cases, say, or a question the group might address through the math activity. If someone in the group is particularly engaged by the seminar task, questions inviting the rest of the group to consider her or his ideas are helpful: "What do you think about what Sonya is saying?"

To help participants focus the case discussions on pertinent subjects, suggest that they cite line numbers in their conversations. This technique draws everyone into the specifics of the cases, focuses the conversation on the mathematical ideas of the children, and helps avoid generalized critiques of classrooms and teaching strategies.

Small-group discussion offers opportunities for the facilitator to monitor group dynamics. How are group members relating to one another? Are all the participants contributing to the discussion? Are participants' ideas being respected?

> *[Interacting with small groups] is not about having a right thing to do, but having a stock of alternatives and knowing when to call on which. Ask questions when the group needs to move, ask questions to understand their thinking, listen to affirm, refer to what you heard to encourage someone to speak, or refer to it because you think they can make a connection that might be useful.*

Listening to the small-group discussions helps you gather information and make decisions about the whole-group discussion to follow. To initiate whole-group discussion, you might choose among several strategies:

- Bring out an issue that caused confusion in small groups: "It seems that lots of people are struggling with [issue X], so I thought we could come together to see if we can sort it out."

- Begin with an idea that some groups found stimulating: "Many of you were discussing [issue Y]. Now I think it would be worth our while to discuss where you agree and where your interpretations and perspectives differ."

- Highlight a point made in one small group that is important for everyone to consider: "David said something that left me thinking . . ."

- Draw the group's attention to an issue that had been ignored in small groups: "As I went from group to group, I heard lots of interesting and important ideas, but I didn't hear anyone talking about [issue Z] . . ."

- For case discussions (print or video), review what one or two children did and then move into one of the focus questions about those children.

The strategy you employ to begin a whole-group discussion depends on the ideas you want to pursue and the issues that arise during small-group time. In general, however, whole-group discussion should not be a simple rehash of what went on in small groups. Its purpose should be to raise discussion to a new level, "to encourage ideas, thoughts, and conjectures to surface for all to grapple with." As the discussion progresses, be attentive to who seems engaged and who might be confused. If necessary, you can slow the pace of discussion and provide time for thinking about and reacting to what is being said by recording, on easel paper or the board, ideas that emerge from the group.

Understanding participants' emotions

People enter the seminar with expectations based on their past staff-development experiences, experiences which may differ from those DMI offers. For example, some participants may feel disappointed that they are not leaving each session with activities for their classrooms. On the other hand, they may feel excited about learning the mathematics for themselves, investigating children's mathematical thinking, or following the development of children's mathematical understanding over time. One participant wrote about how she had to readjust her thinking to appreciate what she was learning:

I compare it to approaching a glass, thinking that you are going to be drinking chocolate milk and ending up drinking tomato juice. At first you are surprised and then you change your mental image and readjust your taste buds.

She explained that once she understood what the seminar would be, she began to enjoy it. ("I do like tomato juice!") She went on to say that she appreciates seeing things in new ways and discovering a better practice for her students.

You may have to tell participants explicitly that the seminar may challenge their present ways of thinking and even their conceptions about what it means to be a good teacher. Feelings of ambivalence or resistance are to be expected.

Early in one of the pilot seminars, a participant wrote about how the course had shaken her confidence, even as it promised a new and enhanced professional identity:

After the first two sessions I asked myself, where were we going? I didn't know. It was then that I started to pay attention to the word "inquiry." I thought I was already doing this. I'd begun to have self-doubts and a feeling of frustration was beginning to build. . . .

My first deduction after three sessions was hmm—I really wasn't paying enough attention to my students' thinking. I was still doing a lot of assuming.

So you are making me think and you're shaking me out of complacency. What do I expect?—to get better at what I do. I think you're taking me down a completely new road.

Although listening carefully to what participants are saying about the seminar is often unsettling, you as facilitator do need to be aware of their questions and frustrations. Attending to participants in this way communicates your concern and respect for them. At times, you may find that small adaptations alleviate their problems. At other times, you may learn that their frustrations are part of the process of learning and do not indicate a problem at all. For example, after reviewing participants' evaluations at the end of her seminar, one facilitator wrote that when respondents gave their overall seminar experience the highest rating, "very valuable," she was pleasantly surprised, "since participants expressed significant frustration, critical questioning, anger, discomfort, and resistance throughout the course."

Because it is not possible or appropriate for all participants to express concerns, questions, and frustrations during seminar discussions, it is useful to have a variety of strategies for keeping in touch with individuals. "Exit cards" are an efficient way of gathering this information. By posing two questions for participants to respond to briefly, in writing, before they leave each session, you can discover what people are learning, what they are concerned about, and what questions they have. Suggestions for exit-card questions for each session are given in the detailed agendas.

Responding to portfolio assignments

Throughout a DMI seminar, participants complete writing assignments that they collect in portfolios. Some assignments encourage teachers to examine the mathematical thinking of their own students; other writings provide a vehicle for participants to articulate and clarify their ideas. Still others help participants reflect on how those ideas are developing over time.

Participants should receive feedback about every assignment from you, the seminar facilitator. How you respond will vary with the type of activity and the goal of that particular seminar session. When the assignment is a personal reflection focused on the participants' own learning or their students' mathematical thinking, individualized written responses to each teacher work well. Another good approach is a single written response to the whole group, summarizing for participants the variety of issues addressed in all the writings. You might then acknowledge people's work orally through comments at the next session; this allows you to recognize individual ideas while also using your summary to move the group into a discussion on these points.

Responding to portfolio assignments is important because it validates the participants' work and indicates your interest in their opinions and ideas. To help you formulate appropriate responses, examples of participants' writing and a facilitator's responses to them are included in "Maxine's Journal."

Supporting all teachers, with any math curriculum

The DMI seminars were not designed as support for a particular elementary or middle school curriculum. Rather, they are intended to help teachers develop mathematical understandings and come to understand children's learning in ways that will enhance their practice, no matter what curriculum they use.

Some teachers who use conventional textbooks have discovered that their new-found insights bring new life to their mathematics teaching. "I have a new and better way of engaging students for the purpose of finding out what they understand so that we can build on that understanding."

Those who use *Standards*-based curricula have reported that their participation in a DMI seminar orients them to the basic approach and deepens their understanding of the mathematics.

A user of *Everyday Mathematics* explained, "I have been using this curriculum for three years and had begun to feel comfortable with it. Now DMI has shown me how to bring my students to a deeper level of understanding."

A user of *MathLand* reported, "Taking a DMI seminar reinforced my belief that learners need to be directly engaged with math ideas. . . . The seminar experience made me more strongly convinced about using the *MathLand* approach in my own classroom."

A user of *Investigations* said, "There are some parts of the curriculum that I had been skipping because I did not see why students needed them. Now for the first time I see why I would want students doing the parts I had been skipping."

Middle school teachers using various curricula have similar things to say. One reported, "This course and these readings have reminded me how important it is to analyze my students' thinking and work. I am always asking, *What do I want students to know and be able to do*? I need to remember to make the time to assess whether they have really learned it. *What have they learned and how do I know*?"

Another wrote, "I am interested in helping students develop their abilities to be creative mathematical thinkers and problem solvers. I am looking for ways to have students pose and investigate rich questions, the way we did in the DMI class. . . . Generally, students have few opportunities to make and justify their own conjectures, to pursue the implications of the different ideas that emerge while they are investigating various concepts. . . . [and so they] learn too well the lesson that mathematics is about finding answers. They aren't sufficiently exposed to another major driving force of mathematics thought and investigation: *posing questions*."

A third offered this: "The DMI course has helped me listen to children's conversations as they work to make sense of key ideas in mathematics. As a middle school teacher, I now better recognize and understand the vast differences in the developmental levels of individual students. The course also led me to observe that as students press forward to make sense of new ideas, they tend to cycle back to touch base with or reexamine the fundamental ideas, the building blocks of mathematical thinking."

Adapting to different formats

The DMI seminars were originally planned for teachers meeting on a weekly or biweekly basis, in three-hour sessions, with eight such sessions for each seminar. However, the materials have been successfully adapted to a variety of formats. Following are comments from facilitators on some of the formats they have used.

Seminar meeting for three hours weekly

"I really like this format. It's very intense, yet enough time between sessions that participants have time to reflect, try things in classrooms, etc. Even when we had two weeks between sessions (because of vacation), participants still admitted to doing the work the night before!"

Seminar meeting for three hours after school, biweekly

"Meeting every other week gave both the participants and the facilitators some time to reflect on the work we were doing. As a facilitator who was at the same time a classroom teacher, it was important for me to have the week between to prepare with my co-facilitators and to reflect on our participants' work. The participants commented that meeting every other week made it seem more manageable, in terms of the amount of time they spent in class. They also liked having time between sessions to try things they had been thinking about."

Seminar meeting for three hours on Saturdays, biweekly

"To my surprise, the teachers don't complain about spending their Saturday mornings this way. In contrast to after-school seminars, they arrive rested and refreshed. We'll meet approximately every other week throughout the year to cover the content of two DMI seminars."

Seminar meeting for 90 minutes weekly

"We chose this format to accommodate child-care issues for the teachers in our school. Having weekly meetings for an entire year seems to maintain a high level of 'mindfulness' about math, individual commitment, and openness to the work; it also offers an invaluable cohesiveness to the group and to our shared purpose. The drawback is that the case discussions and the math activities that support examination of the cases do not take place in the same session."

Seminar meeting for 90 minutes biweekly

"This format encourages participation by teachers who are involved in numerous after-school activities or who have young children at home. One disadvantage is that it spreads each session over a month; I'm now feeling the need to move more quickly. It's also not possible, at this pace, to complete more than one seminar in a single school year unless you add some sessions at other times."

Each seminar covered in four full-day workshops

"Teachers who participated in the four full-day meetings explained that, because of child-care issues and other concerns, they would have been unable to attend after-school meetings. They said they liked the feeling of shedding their teaching responsibilities in the morning, to have the experience of being the student all day. And they liked the intensity. Issues to think about include how to cover teachers' classrooms, how to rearrange the agendas, and selecting from all the homework assignments."

Summer school course, three and a half hours, twice a week

"I taught a summer school course that met twice a week, for three and a half hours each session, over a four-week period (though it should have been longer). I didn't follow the DMI agendas exactly. . . . Students read two or three cases for each class and, as much as possible, I posed problems for the class to try before they were asked to read about what the children did. I also selected particular focus questions for students to read, think, and write about before the case discussions."

Summer institute, 10 full days (for two seminars)

"We scheduled sessions so the institute did not meet on two afternoons. Participants were told ahead of time that for these afternoons, they could make appointments with children for specific work related to the mathematics of the seminar. On other days we scheduled long lunch breaks, giving teachers enough time to reread the cases we would be discussing in the afternoon. Although teachers could not be testing new ideas in their classrooms as the seminar progressed, the concentration and immersion into the work was a positive."

Semester course for undergraduates

"In keeping with the structure of our college schedule, DMI for undergraduates met for 14 weeks, twice a week. That gave us 28 sessions, each 75 minutes long—enough time to do the work of two seminars. Students had a reading assignment and a portfolio assignment due each week."

Working with different constituencies

The DMI seminars address fundamental issues of mathematics education: understanding *what* students are to learn and *how* they learn it. Although the materials were initially written for use with practicing teachers, other constituencies concerned about the same issues—including undergraduates, school administrators, and parents—have

benefited from DMI seminars as well. In the following paragraphs, facilitators of some of these seminars describe the approaches they took.

DMI as an undergraduate course

"We followed the DMI curriculum closely, modifying the timing of the agendas to fit the college schedule. Weekly requirements included a reading assignment from the casebook and a portfolio entry. Each student was paired with a local teacher who has been particularly reflective about his or her own practice, to provide access to classrooms for the portfolio assignments. The only modification made to the portfolio assignments was to eliminate those requiring the collection and analysis of student work."

DMI as professional development for teacher educators, staff developers, and teacher-leaders

"Participants in this seminar engaged with the materials at many different levels. For some, the bulk of their attention was given to analyzing student thinking and working on their own mathematics. For others, participating in DMI activities provided an opportunity to reflect on goals for teachers' professional development and to analyze how the different activities are designed to achieve those goals. In addition, 'Maxine's Journal' was used as a case to inquire into issues of facilitation and teacher learning."

From pilot work with the DMI seminars on Number and Operations, there is evidence that the curriculum can also be adapted for use with administrators and parents.

Visiting the DMI web site

The Education Development Center (EDC) maintains a web site with information about the DMI curriculum:

http://www.edc.org/LTT/CDT/DMIcur.html

Along with links related to other projects from EDC's Center for the Development of Teaching, you will find information on studies being done related to the use and impact of these professional development seminars. The link "Advice from DMI Users" leads to pages where facilitators who have used these materials share some of their reflections, strategies, and discoveries. The site also provides information about DMI Leadership Institutes designed for staff developers, teacher educators, teacher-leaders, and others who support teachers' professional development in K–7 mathematics.

Bibliography

Seminar participants or facilitators may find it helpful to refer to supplemental readings that address particular concerns or interests related to issues raised by this DMI seminar. The following are suggested references.

Burns, M. & Tank, B. (1988). *A collection of math lessons from grades 1 through 3.* Sausalito, CA: Math Solutions Publications.

Burns, M. (1987). *A collection of math lessons from grades 3 through 6.* Sausalito, CA: Math Solutions Publications.

These collections offer exemplary classroom activities across a range of mathematics content, including number sense, geometry, measurement, data, and probability. For each lesson, the authors provide a detailed account of the lesson as it unfolded in a classroom with commentary on what the students did, where they got stuck, and how the teacher built on the students' work to create the next lesson. Throughout are useful teacher reflections—what she's noticing about the children's thinking, and why she makes certain instructional decisions.

For more extended units on particular topics, look at the *Math by All Means* series of units, also published by Math Solutions. These include *Place Value* (grade 2), *Geometry* (grade 2), *Geometry* (grade 3), *Multiplication* (grade 3), *Division* (grades 3–4), and *Area and Perimeter* (grades 5–6).

Duckworth, E. (1987). *The having of wonderful ideas and other essays on teaching and learning.* New York: Teachers College Press.

Eleanor Duckworth, a well-known educator and student of children's thinking, has collected many of her essays in this volume. The essays consider a range of issues in teaching and learning in a variety of content areas, including mathematics, science, and language. Each essay provides an opportunity for educators to think more deeply about their practice as they consider the author's belief that "the having of wonderful ideas is the essence of intellectual development."

Heaton, R. (2000). *Teaching mathematics to the new standards: Relearning the dance.* New York: Teachers College Press.

As an experienced elementary school teacher, Ruth Heaton set out to learn to teach mathematics for understanding. With honesty and courage, she lets us in on her journey to invent a new practice, sharing with us her confusions, struggles, successes, and discoveries.

Hiebert, J., Carpenter, T., Fennema, E., Fuson, K., Wearne, D., Murray, H., Olivier, A., & Human, P. (1997). *Making sense: Teaching and learning mathematics with understanding*. Portsmouth, NH: Heinemann.

This book is based on the authors' work in four separate research programs, all of which investigated the effects of new instructional approaches in the teaching of mathematics. Out of their ongoing discussion, a consensus emerged about what features are essential to support students' mathematical understandings. By describing these features and offering pictures of several classrooms that exhibit them, the authors create a framework within which elementary teachers can reflect on their own practice and think about what it means to teach for understanding.

Mokros, J. (1996). *Beyond facts and flashcards: Exploring math with your kids*. Portsmouth, NH: Heinemann.

This book is both a resource and a consumer's guide to mathematics learning for parents of elementary school children. Its aims are to build parents' understanding of, and demand for, solid mathematics education for their children and to encourage the incorporation of real mathematics into everyday family activities. The book gives extended examples of how parents can make changes: by learning what mathematics really is and solving mathematical problems for themselves; by tuning into the mathematics that interests their children; and by doing mathematics with their children the same way that they read, ride bikes, or make music with them—with a sense of adventure, surprise, challenge, and togetherness.

Mokros, J., Russell, S. J., & Economopoulos, K. (1995). *Beyond arithmetic: Changing mathematics in the elementary classroom*. Parsippany, NJ: Dale Seymour Publications.

Elementary teachers have many questions about current efforts to transform mathematics instruction: Why does the approach advocated by the reform movement give less attention to algorithms and procedures that have formed the backbone of traditional mathematics instruction? Will children really learn important mathematical ideas, and be prepared for their futures, if we radically change the nature of mathematics instruction? Is it worth the risk? This book is aimed at helping teachers grapple with these issues and figure out how to begin to transform their teaching. Topics include the role of innovative curriculum materials, new modes of assessment, what a reform classroom looks like, talking with parents, and answers to common questions teachers ask.

National Council of Teachers of Mathematics. (2000). *Principles and standards for school mathematics*. Reston, VA: Author.

One of the key documents in the current effort to reform mathematics education, *Principles and Standards* "extends the vision of NCTM's original *Standards* documents and . . . offers vision and direction for school mathematics programs. The Principles set forth important characteristics of mathematics programs, and the Standards discuss the mathematics that students need to know and be able to do across the grades. The grade-band chapters (preK–2, 3–5, 6–8, 9–12) provide both specific expectations for those grades and a plethora of engaging examples to bring those ideas to life" [*NCTM News Bulletin*, April, 2000]. The document also discusses how these principles and standards can be implemented and what it will take to support excellent mathematics teaching and learning in our schools.

Ohanian, S. (1992). *Garbage pizza, patchwork quilts, and math magic.* New York: W. H. Freeman.

The author, a teacher and freelance writer, traveled to schools across the country and documented the changes she saw happening in elementary mathematics classes. She recounts stories of teachers and students engaging in exciting mathematics and writes about such critical issues as the administrator-teacher partnership and communicating with parents.

Parker, R. (1993). *Mathematical power: Lessons from a classroom.* Portsmouth, NH: Heinemann.

In this complex, realistic picture of a fifth-grade class whose teacher tries to realize the goals set by the NCTM *Standards*, we see the teacher and her mentor select mathematics activities that will promote what they want their students to learn, establish a climate of inquiry in the classroom, and figure out what it means to teach and learn mathematics. A section on assessment and the use of portfolios is included.

Rowan, T., & Bourne, B. (1994). *Thinking like mathematicians: Putting the K–4 NCTM Standards into practice.* Portsmouth, NH: Heinemann.

In this book the authors consider, from a developmental perspective, children's construction of mathematical meaning. As they describe implementation of the NCTM *Standards* in grades K–4, they offer vignettes that highlight children's thinking and illustrate mathematics teaching and learning in several classrooms. The book ends with a chapter of questions and answers about implementing the NCTM *Standards* in the classroom.

Schifter, D., & Fosnot, C. T. (1993). *Reconstructing mathematics education: Stories of teachers meeting the challenge of reform*. New York: Teachers College Press.

Case studies of teachers show the struggles, doubts, and successes they experience as they work to *change* their mathematics instruction. Descriptions of classrooms include second graders hypothesizing about even and odd numbers, third graders demonstrating the commutativity of multiplication, and sixth graders puzzling over the mysteries of fractions. In each situation, the authors consider the teacher's intentions in designing the activity, the instructional decisions she makes as the children engage in it, and her reflections afterward. This book is particularly recommended for those who want to learn more about emotional aspects of teacher change.

Schifter, D. (Ed.). (1996). *What's happening in math class? Volume 1: Envisioning new practices through teacher narratives*. New York: Teachers College Press.

Schifter, D. (Ed.). (1996). *What's happening in math class? Volume 2: Reconstructing professional identities*. New York: Teachers College Press.

The two volumes of *What's Happening in Math Class?* contain 22 reflective, first-person narratives written by K–12 classroom teachers and nine essays by teacher educators. Volume 1 explores how the principles of mathematics education reform are put into play in day-to-day classroom life. It takes on such issues as establishing a community of inquiry in an elementary classroom and reaching *all* students. Volume 2 examines the experience of change and growth as teachers take on new roles in transforming their practice, including the history of a mathphobic sixth-grade teacher who confronts her fears and moves beyond.

Stiff, L. V., & Curcio, F. R. (Eds.). (1999). *Developing mathematics reasoning in grades K–12: 1999 Yearbook*. Reston, VA: National Council of Teachers of Mathematics.

This NCTM *Yearbook* contains chapters that address mathematical reasoning at the elementary-, middle-, and high-school levels in various content areas. Chapters by Susan Jo Russell and Deborah Schifter discuss particular video and print cases excerpted from the DMI Number and Operations seminars.

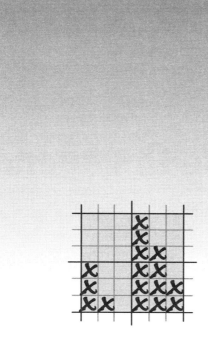

Detailed Agendas

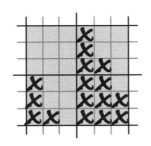

How to Use the Agendas

When I started co-facilitating a DMI seminar with a colleague, I felt glued to the facilitator's guide. I'd prepare for a session by reading the sections I was responsible for and trying to figure out how I was going to remember to say everything that was in the guide. In fact, I remember clutching the guide during a few early sessions as I facilitated discussions so that I wouldn't forget anything. Then I had the chance to meet with other people piloting the material and we talked about this. I was relieved to hear other people were having those feelings. The discussion turned to how do you make the material your own, really own it, yet keep the original intent of it intact. I thought about that for a long time. Instead of trying to memorize what the guide said, that became my focus when planning for a session.

— a DMI facilitator

After the first few sessions of DMI, I was feeling a little uncomfortable. It seemed like I was marching through the agenda as outlined without seeing connections. There never seemed to be enough time to do the experiences, and we'd stop one to move on to another. That didn't feel right to me, but since it was my first time facilitating a seminar, I thought it was important to follow the guide. But then two amazing things happened. I realized that the same issues about [the mathematics] were coming up repeatedly, and had been coming up all along. It didn't really matter if we were doing a math activity, discussing the cases, or watching the video, the conversation continued to be about important mathematical ideas and how the children were thinking about those ideas. I also realized that the agenda was a helpful guide, but because the conversations from one activity or session to the next revolved around the same ideas, it was OK not to feel closure for every experience. We could move on, accomplish our work, and I could feel confident that questions raised would be addressed in future sessions.

— a DMI facilitator

The Developing Mathematical Ideas seminars support teachers as they explore the mathematics of the elementary curriculum for themselves and examine the way children develop mathematical ideas across the grades. Each seminar coordinates the discussion of print and video cases with a variety of other activities: mathematical explorations for adults, investigations of the mathematical thinking done by seminar participants' own students, analyses of activities from innovative curricula, and readings about related research.

The detailed agendas in this guide describe a sequence of activities for each DMI seminar session, with a suggested time allotment for each activity. A preparation and materials section alerts facilitators to the supplies, handouts, and equipment needed for each session.

Included with the agendas are handouts ready to be duplicated for participants, including focus questions that guide the case discussions, mathematics activities to be done during the sessions, and the homework assignments that participants are to complete outside of the seminar sessions.

Format and timing

The facilitator's guide lays out a plan for covering *Working with Data* in eight sessions that meet for three hours each. However, facilitators have conducted DMI seminars in other configurations.

For example, one facilitator conducted the sessions over five full-day meetings, using half a day for each session, which left two additional half-days for participants to work together on their data projects, since they were attending from a large geographical area. Another facilitator started the seminar with a full-day meeting for Session 1 and 2, and followed with six 3-hour after-school sessions.

Some facilitators have added a session solely for work on data projects. In some cases, they were available to meet with groups during this time; in other cases, they simply left the classroom space open for participant use. It is, however, important to note that many facilitators do *not* provide extra class time for project work, and are simply clear and firm that this work must be done outside of class.

Trying to follow the suggested time allotment for each activity—for example, a 40-minute case discussion, a 25-minute videotape, and a 30-minute math activity—may seem to fragment the session. However, the mathematical theme of the session provides coherence; ideas that emerge during one activity are revisited in another. In general, you should follow the suggested timing of the activities rather than expand one at the expense of another. For example, if participants want to continue a case discussion beyond the time allotted, it is likely that the mathematical issues that are engaging them in the cases will also be addressed through the next activity. In such a situation, you could acknowledge that you see the participants are doing some important thinking and assure them that turning to this new activity will allow them to continue their discussions. On the other hand, if the discussion of the cases feels finished before the allotted time, you might end it and make more time for the next activity.

Facilitators have reported how important it was for them to develop a sense of the intention of each session and of the DMI seminar as a whole. Examining the issues raised in the overviews to each chapter in the casebook and reading "Maxine's Journal" can provide a starting point for this understanding. As you prepare for the session, consider what you want your group to get from each activity and how that learning contributes to the overall goal of the session.

Once you know what you want to accomplish in each session, you will be able to use the agenda suggestions flexibly to suit your purposes.

DMI seminar activities

Certain types of activities occur in every session; others may come up just once or twice in the entire seminar. Facilitators should be prepared to handle all of the following activities.

Reading and discussing the print cases

The first seven chapters of the *Working with Data* casebook contain case studies. The introductory text in each chapter describes that set of cases and highlights the general mathematical themes addressed. Participants are expected to read both the introductory text and the set of cases before the seminar meeting. Remind participants to consider the issues raised by the chapter overview as they read and discuss the cases. Since each case has something significant to offer, all the cases should be read and considered.

To guide the case discussion, distribute the appropriate set of focus questions (a handout) just before the discussion begins. These focus questions often refer to only a subset of the cases, drawing participants' attention to very specific issues. Once those have been addressed, groups often find it useful to consider the entire set of cases while revisiting the more general questions posed in the chapter overview.

Sometimes participants wonder why the focus questions aren't given out for homework to help them structure their reading of the cases. It can be helpful to explain that while the questions are useful for focusing the group's discussion, having them ahead of time could limit participants' reading. The chapter as a whole provides a broader view of the mathematical issues across grade levels that they will be drawing on for all their work in the seminar.

Viewing and discussing the video cases

In some of the DMI seminar sessions, you will be showing video cases of children working on mathematics problems. While the mathematics work seen in the video is often similar to that in the print cases, the videos bring the children to life in a way that is difficult to capture in print. The children mumble, fidget, write messily, and speak haltingly as they work to express their mathematical ideas. After seeing the video cases, participants often remark that they can better "hear" the students' voices when they read the print cases. Running times and summaries for each video segment are included in the agendas.

Working on the mathematics activities

The mathematics activities offer work with the mathematical ideas that are addressed in the print and video cases, at a level that is appropriate and challenging for adult learners. Sometimes the mathematics investigation precedes the case discussion; other times, it follows the discussion of children's work. If you are adjusting the agendas to fit a different format, be sure the order of the activities is appropriate.

Participants are sometimes uncomfortable because their mathematics work in a DMI seminar leaves them confused about something they thought they understood. This can be especially unsettling if it appears that the discussion for that topic is over. Reassure participants that the ideas raised in one session are revisited in another, and that future sessions will include further opportunities to work on the mathematical issues they find confusing, troubling, or puzzling. At the same time it is important to acknowledge that, although closure is reached for some ideas, the work always raises new questions and there is always more to think about.

Exploring innovative curriculum materials

During each seminar, participants examine lessons or activities drawn from one of several elementary mathematics curricula. For homework, participants familiarize themselves with the activities. Then in the seminar session, they meet in small groups to discuss how they would use the material to support their students' thinking. The content of the suggested lessons is related to the mathematical issues they have been discussing.

Suggestions for this seminar include activities from *Everyday Math* (Everyday Learning), *Investigations* (Scott Foresman), *Math Trailblazers* (Kendell/ Hunt Publishing), and *MathLand* (Creative Publications).

If you are working in or with a school system that has adopted one of these curricula, it will be beneficial for your group to study the suggested activities from that curriculum. If your system is in the process of choosing a curriculum, you may want to explore several possibilities. If your system already has an established curriculum other than those that are listed, you might look for related activities to explore in that resource.

The curriculum activities are *not* included in this facilitator's guide; you will need to locate the relevant material for participant use. An effort was made to suggest activities that require minimal preparation time for facilitators and that use manipulative materials commonly available. The suggested activity list appears with the agenda for Session 4; if you anticipate needing extra time to obtain the activities you want your group to explore, turn to this list early to begin preparing for that session.

Reading and discussing the research highlights essay

The last chapter of the casebook for *Working with Data* is an essay that describes research findings related to the mathematical issues raised by the cases. Throughout the essay, the research results are explicated with examples from those cases. Reading and discussing the essay allows participants to consider the overall themes of the casebook and to get a broader perspective on the issues raised by individual cases.

The spirit of inquiry fostered in the case discussions should also be applied to the research essay. That is, participants should feel free to question and challenge the ideas put forward and to compare these ideas with their own experiences. At the same time, they should be encouraged to challenge their own assumptions and beliefs by comparing them to the research findings.

In other DMI seminars, the research essay is the focus of the final session, after all the cases have been read and discussed. However, in the testing of *Working with Data*, facilitators found that participants' efforts for the last class were concentrated on presenting their data projects, and they were not also able to give the research essay the time and attention it needs. Sharing of final projects needs to remain in Session 8; it is an important culminating activity, and participants generally need as much time as possible to complete their project. For this reason, discussion of the research essay for *Working with Data* moves to Session 7, leaving a lighter reading load (the last set of cases) for Session 8.

Discussing portfolio assignments

In addition to their reading assignments in the casebook, participants are expected to complete writing assignments and keep these in their portfolios. Some assignments ask teachers to reflect on their learning in the seminar or to discuss implications of that learning for their teaching practice. Through other assignments, participants investigate the thinking of their *own* students. When appropriate, seminar time is allotted for discussion and analysis of participants' written work.

When participants are sharing their writing about their own classes and their own students, be aware that this activity makes some participants anxious. You need to clearly establish that the discussions of one another's writing are *not* to be critiques of any teacher's practice or writing, but rather opportunities for the group to examine the mathematical thinking of the students. For this work, participants meet in small groups and are asked to read through each other's papers before starting any discussion. As participants become more familiar with the process of writing about their students' mathematics, they grow in their ability to use these assignments to deepen their own thinking. When they first begin, teachers may be uncomfortable sharing what went wrong in their lessons or owning up to being confused by their own students. Encourage participants to use their writing as a way to work on something they are trying to figure out. Point out that when they bring their writing to the seminar, they will have a chance to get reactions from like-minded colleagues.

You will also be reinforcing this in your written responses to participants after they have turned in their papers. "Maxine's Journal" includes samples of participants' writing and the facilitator's responses to give you some ideas about what participants should hear from you.

Using exit cards

The portfolio assignments give facilitators a sense of how individual participants are engaging with the ideas of the seminar, but there is usually a time lag between when they are written and when facilitators read them. Therefore, the DMI agendas allot 5 minutes at the end of each session for participants to provide more immediate feedback using "exit cards."

Facilitators have found it effective to choose two or three prompts for each session to guide participant responses. These can be written on easel paper or read aloud. Passing out an index card to each participant just before posting or reading the prompts helps to make clear that this is *not* an optional activity, but rather an important conclusion to every session. Some facilitators prefer to use NCR (no carbon required) paper instead of index cards for exit card cards for exit-card responses. This allows participants to keep a copy of their comments. Exit-card prompts are suggested in the agendas, or you may want to devise questions to get at issues relevant to your particular group.

Preparation for the seminar

In preparation for the *Working with Data* seminar, send a letter to seminar participants so that they receive it at least two weeks before the first meeting. Include any necessary information about logistics. It is useful for participants to have a pad of graph paper for homework and for use in class. Also send the two-page handout (following), which explains the preseminar assignment that participants are to complete and bring to the first session.

WORKING WITH DATA

First Homework

This assignment is to be completed before the first session of this seminar. At that first session, we will be reading and talking about the first part of the portfolio assignment, and we will be discussing the casebook reading. You will hand in the second part of the portfolio assignment at the first meeting.

Portfolio assignment 1: Key ideas about data

In this seminar, you'll be learning about ideas in data. Write the questions you have about teaching and learning about data. Your questions will likely change over the course of the seminar, but for now, what questions and thoughts are you coming in with? What are you currently thinking is important for your students to learn about data?

Portfolio assignment 2: Working with data

On the next page is a set of data, reported from School District A and School District B, about the number of years the elementary teachers in each district have been teaching in grades K–6. Your task is to represent these data in some way that helps you see what is going on. Describe in writing what you notice about the data and how the data are similar or different for the two districts.

Don't worry if this task is unfamiliar to you. If you are not sure how to approach the problem, do what you can, then explain what's confusing, puzzling, or unfamiliar about the problem.

Reading assignment: Starting the casebook

Read the introduction to the casebook, *Working with Data*. Then read all of chapter 1, the introductory text as well as cases 1–3.

Data for portfolio assignment 2

Find a way to represent these data. What do you notice about the data? How are the data for the two districts similar or different?

Number of years teaching in K–6	Number of teachers in District A	Number of teachers in District B
1		
2	1	1
3	2	3
4	1	1
5	1	2
6	5	2
7		3
8		
9	1	3
10		1
11		3
12		2
13	3	3
14	1	1
15	4	
16	4	3
17	2	1
18	4	2
19	4	4
20	3	2
21	2	
22	3	
23	1	
24		
25	1	4

Getting Started with Data

Session Agenda

Sharing homework (key ideas)	Groups of three	15 minutes
Introductions	Whole group	20 minutes
Math activity ("A Data Investigation")	Groups of four Whole group	30 minutes 15 minutes
Break and orientation		20 minutes
Case discussion	Groups of three Whole group	25 minutes 20 minutes
Viewing the video ("Pocket Data")	Whole group	25 minutes
Homework and exit cards	Whole group	10 minutes

Background Preparation

Read
- the casebook, "Introduction" and chapter 1
- "Maxine's Journal," Goals for the Seminar (p. 121) and Session 1 (p. 125)
- the agenda for Session 1

Preview
- the video segment for Session 1

Materials

Prepare
- a large copy of the line plot from Olivia's case 3, on easel paper or the board (see the Focus Questions, p. 33)
- a large copy of the line plot from the video segment for Session 1 (see the video summary, p. 30)

Materials (continued)

Duplicate
- "Math Activity: A Data Investigation" (p. 32)
- "Focus Questions: Chapter 1" (p. 33)
- "The Portfolio Process" (p. 34)
- "If You Have to Miss a Class…"(p. 35)
- "Second Homework" (p. 36)

Obtain
- small index cards for data collection
- unlined easel paper
- markers, rulers, yardsticks
- tape or glue sticks
- small box or tray for each math activity group (optional)
- VCR
- large index cards or NCR paper (for exit cards)

Agenda

Sharing homework
(15 minutes)

The first activity of the seminar is designed to move participants immediately into the ideas they will be working on together. As individuals enter the room, arrange them in groups of three and tell them to read and discuss one another's lists of initial questions and thoughts about data (portfolio assignment 1). Consider organizing the groups so that people from different schools have a chance to interact. You can let them know there will be time later in the session for introductions and orientation.

Write out the agenda for the entire session and the directions for this first activity on the board or easel so that participants will be able to see the whole plan. Opening the seminar in this fashion lets everyone know the sessions will begin promptly at the announced time. Point out that they will have a total of 15 minutes for this activity, and remind them to be sure that everyone in their group has some time to share.

Introductions
(20 minutes)

Have everyone introduce themselves—names, positions, schools. Encourage participants to learn each other's names. For the first few sessions, they should introduce themselves every time they work in a small group.

Say a few words about the seminar and your own goals. Since many participants come to this work in data with memories of negative experiences in statistics courses, you may want to spend a few minutes asking about participants' previous experiences with and feelings about working with data. Ask participants to share briefly with the whole group a few ideas that came up in their small-group discussion. What thoughts and questions are on their minds as they begin this course?

Math activity
(45 minutes)

Groups of four (30 minutes)

Whole group (15 minutes)

Participants collect and organize data about themselves in response to the question, *With what well-known person would you like to have a conversation?*

They will be working with categorical data and noticing how these data can be organized in different ways to give different views of the data.

Provide each participant with small index cards for recording their answer to the question. Each participant needs as many cards as there are small groups.

For the data collection step, participants individually choose a well-known person they would like to have a conversation with. The person can be real or fictional, living or dead, but should be a public figure from history, literature, politics, or the like, not a personal friend or relative. It isn't necessary that everyone immediately recognize the name, but that person should have had some recognized impact on or place in the world. Don't spend lots of time discussing who can be included; participants can use their judgment.

Each participant writes his or her choice on several index cards so that each small group can collect a card from each person. For distribution, participants might place their index cards in a separate pile (or box or tray) for each group. Small groups should each end up with a set that includes one card from every seminar participant.

Participants then work in small groups to discuss and represent the collected data, following the steps on the math activity handout. Provide each group of four with copies of the handout, easel paper, markers, rulers, yardsticks, and tape or glue sticks. As you walk around and interact with the small groups, help them focus on using these data to find something out about the whole class group. If any names on the cards are unfamiliar, groups should feel free to ask questions so they can successfully categorize the people. Clearly limit the time small groups have to develop their categories to about 20 minutes.

Display the completed posters for whole-group discussion. Give participants a few minutes to look at them. Then ask each group to mention one or two issues that came up. The point is not to get a "report" from each group about what they did; rather, focus on issues they wrestled with in organizing and describing the data. You might ask:

1. What issues came up for you as you tried to represent these data?

2. What do the data tell us about our group?

3. What questions arise for you while looking at these data? How might you modify the survey to get at your own questions?

Break and orientation

(20 minutes)

Just before or after the 15-minute break, take 5 minutes to explain any seminar logistics. Distribute the "Portfolio Process" handout and answer participants' questions about maintaining a portfolio. The portfolio can be a folder, a binder, or any means of keeping a collection of their written work and your responses to it. Explain how important reading and responding to their papers is for you as the seminar facilitator, because knowing their thinking helps you plan for each session. They should understand that the portfolio assignments are carefully designed to move their ideas forward and will often be used as the basis for class discussions. Establish a routine for collecting and returning assignments.

Distribute the handout "If You Have to Miss a Class…" or orally explain your expectations about attendance. Emphasize that the ideas of the seminar build from session to session and that missing any session can jeopardize their continued understanding and active participation in class activities, unless they make efforts to catch up on the work they've missed.

Case discussion   (45 minutes)

Groups of three (25 minutes)

Whole group (20 minutes)

The first chapter of the casebook provides images of children across the grades as they are beginning to make sense of data.

In this seminar, cases are sometimes used to focus on children's thinking and sometimes to explore the mathematics content. The focus questions for this first set of cases encourage participants to do both. Questions 1 and 3 direct attention to the students' thinking, while question 2 asks participants to describe and analyze a set of numerical data. The cases and the participants' math work are concerned with both categorical and numerical data, so they should begin to distinguish between these two types. They will need to understand this distinction as they begin to plan their data projects for the next homework. (Refer to the Data Terms section, p. 110, for more information on different types of data.)

For this case discussion, explain that small groups will have approximately 25 minutes to work on the focus questions; then everyone will gather for a whole-group discussion based on their conversations. The wording of question 1 encourages participants to point to specific evidence in the cases to support their statements about a child's thinking. As you listen to the small-group discussions, help participants ground their ideas in the specifics of the cases, citing by line number the evidence for their ideas. Also be aware of the time remaining for discussion and, if necessary, suggest that a group move on to the next question.

For the whole-group discussion, ask groups to share some of the children's statements they chose for question 1. Then focus on Olivia's case 3. With the data posted on the board or easel paper, ask for comments on what Olivia's students noticed about the data.

Close the discussion by asking participants to consider what is similar and what is different between the displays they made for the math activity (data on well-known people) and the line plot from Olivia's case. This discussion will help clarify differences between categorical and numerical data.

Viewing the video   (25 minutes)

This video shows a complete data collection activity in a second-grade class. Even though there will be little time to discuss the video during this session, showing the video serves an important purpose. It gives participants an image in real time of students collecting, representing, and discussing data. The video clip, which runs a little more than 18 minutes, also shows that data activities do not necessarily have to be long, multiple-session projects—an impression that some participants may have. From the video, participants get ideas about how to approach such an activity when they try one in their own classroom (for homework) before the next session. If there is time, you can ask participants to discuss what they noticed in the video. What are some important features of what's happening in this classroom? Note that a portion of this video will be viewed and discussed at greater length in Session 4.

Homework and exit cards   (10 minutes)

Distribute the "Second Homework" handout and have participants read the portfolio assignment. The video, as an example of a relatively quick data activity, provides a good lead-in to the homework. Participants will be sharing their writing with a small group during the next session, so remind them to bring three copies to share.

Also spend a few minutes explaining the data project described on the homework handout. This data project is to be done outside of class and presented at the last class session. Participants will need to form pairs or small groups and to come up with a question that will result in numerical data (that is, data that are quantities, such as the family-size data in Olivia's case 3). They'll be getting more information on what to do in subsequent sessions. Before the next session, they just need to think of some questions they might be interested in pursuing.

Spend a few minutes talking about exit cards. At the end of each session, you will ask participants to respond to two questions. Sometimes, the questions will focus on participants' own learning, sometimes on issues about children's learning, sometimes on participants' experiences as a member of the seminar. Participants are to answer either on index cards (question 1 on one side, question 2 on the other) or NCR paper. (If you have NCR paper, participants will be able to turn in one copy to you and keep a copy for their portfolio.) Explain that what they write helps you plan for the next session and understand more about what each person is thinking.

Write today's two questions on the board or easel paper:

1. Write about your experience as a participant in the seminar.

2. What issues are on your mind about data analysis?

Before the next session . . .

In preparation for the next session, you need to read and respond to the first homework that participants turned in—their writing about their initial thoughts and questions about data, and their representations of the two school districts' data on years of teaching experience. For more information, see the section in "Maxine's Journal" on responding to the first homework (p. 133).

SESSION 1

Video Summary

Working with Data

Pocket Data, 18 minutes 30 seconds

In this segment, we join a second-grade class in which the students are counting their pockets in response to the survey question posed by the teacher, *How many pockets do you have?* As students report their counts to the teacher, she records them on a line plot on the board. During the recording, they find and correct a couple of miscounts, changing the data to reflect the correct counts.

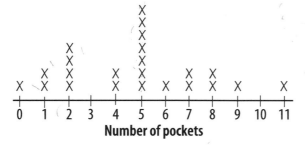

The teacher then asks the students what they notice about the data. Denise says, "I noticed that 5 has a lot." The teacher says, "If 5 has a lot, what does that tell us about our group?" There is a long silence. The teacher waits, and several hands go up. The teacher keeps the conversation focused on Denise's statement, and several students try to articulate what the statement tells about the class.

The teacher asks if there are other observations. Students notice that no people have 3 or 10 pockets, and that there are "ties" between 1, 4, 7, and 8—two people have each of these values. In clarifying this last statement, Alan tries to sort out which numbers are pockets and which are people.

The teacher asks what the range is. Carolyn says the range is 0 to 11. The discussion ends as Destiny points out that they had predicted that 5 would have the most, and it does. The students point out that most jeans have 5 pockets, so this result makes sense to them.

Math Activity: A Data Investigation

With what well-known person would you like to have a conversation?

1. You will be working in small groups on a data investigation. The first step is to decide individually how you would answer the survey question above. Write your response on a separate index card for each small group (including your own).

2. Gather response cards from everyone so that you have a full class set of data for discussion in your small group.

3. *Before looking at the data*, spend a few minutes discussing what might be interesting about them.

4. As a group, sort the data in two different ways, each containing at least three categories.

5. Choose one of your ideas for sorting and arrange your index cards on a large sheet of paper to show that classification.

6. Write a sentence or two on your display that tells what you notice about the data.

7. Post your display on the wall. If you finish before other groups, discuss issues about data that arose for you as you did this activity.

Focus Questions: Chapter 1

Cases 1–3

1. As a group, look through Alexandra's and Beverly's cases. Identify, by line number, statements made by at least five different children that you think bring up important ideas or issues about collecting, representing, or describing data. Be ready to share these statements in the whole-group discussion and tell what issues they raised for you.

2. In Olivia's case 3, consider the data about family size:

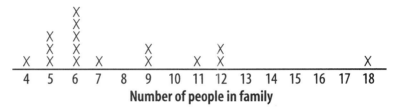
Number of people in family

As a group, write down a few statements that describe the data. What did your group notice as the most important features of this data set?

3. Now consider the students' work in Olivia's case.

a. Lauren, Tyrone, and Jacob wrote two statements on their graph (Figure 2, p. 15, and lines 262–263). What do you think they meant?

b. Look at Inez, Isaac, and Samuel's representation and the discussion about their work (begins at line 276). What important issues about data come up in this part of the discussion?

c. What do Lacey's comments about gaps (line 327) add to an understanding of the data?

d. The data in the first two cases can be put into categories (*bag lunch, school lunch; yes, no, sometimes*). How do the data considered in Olivia's case differ from the data in the first two cases? What kinds of statements that students make about this data set couldn't be made about the data in the other two cases?

The Portfolio Process

As a participant in the DMI seminar *Working with Data*, you will complete writing, reading, and sometimes math assignments for each session. In fact, you already did the first of these in the first homework, when you wrote about questions and thoughts you have about data, worked with the data set from School Districts A and B, and read the cases in the first chapter of the casebook.

For each class session, you will either write a reflective paper or do some work on your data project. Some of your writing will be read and considered in group discussions; all will be a way to communicate with the facilitator of the seminar. The facilitator will collect homework papers during each session. At the following session, your paper will be returned to you with a written response from the facilitator. Please save both your writing and these responses in a folder that will serve as your seminar portfolio.

The purpose of these assignments is to stimulate your thinking. The portfolio will be a record of your work in the seminar and will also serve as a tool for reflection. Particularly toward the end of the seminar, you will be able to look back over your work and think about how your ideas have developed.

If You Have to Miss a Class...

DMI seminar sessions are highly interactive, providing many opportunities for you to express your own ideas and to listen to the ideas of your colleagues. Much of what you learn in the seminar is developed through small-group and whole-group discussions. You will get the most from the seminar, and will contribute positively to the learning of everyone in the group, if you make every effort to prepare for each session and to attend for its full duration.

Frequently, ideas that we introduce in one session are expanded upon and developed more fully in later sessions. Thus, every session is important. If you find that you are unable to attend a particular session or might miss a part of a seminar (by coming late or leaving early), please contact the facilitator as soon as possible. Make arrangements to turn in assignments and to obtain copies of the assignments that you will miss.

When you are absent, you are also responsible for turning in a reflective paper, describing your reaction to the cases we discussed in the session you missed. (This is in addition to the regularly assigned written work.) You also need to turn in your work on any math activity that we completed while you were absent. If at all possible, meet with a classmate to discuss the session you were not able to attend.

Please know that these requirements are designed to minimize loss of learning due to absence.

Second Homework

NOTE: You may find it useful to have a pad of graph paper, both for your work during class and between class sessions. Centimeter or quarter-inch paper works well.

Reading assignment: Casebook chapter 2

Read chapter 2 in the casebook for *Working with Data*, including both the introductory text and cases 4–6.

Portfolio assignment: Examples of student thinking

It is likely that reading the cases, viewing the video, and working on the math in this seminar have made you curious about how your own students think about some of these ideas about data. This assignment asks you to examine the thinking of your own students.

Do a short data activity with your students. Write a few paragraphs about what you did, what the students said and did, and what issues came up for you about your students' thinking. What did you expect? Were you surprised? What did you learn? What questions do you have now? Include specific examples of student work or dialogue in your writing.

At our next session, you will have the chance to share this writing with two other colleagues, so please bring three copies of your writing to class.

Math assignment: Data project

For the next session, think about ideas for a question that could lead to a data investigation you would like to do with a partner or small group of seminar participants. The questions might relate to some issue about education, about your school or community, or just something that interests you. Come next time with at least two questions you might want to pursue. Keep in mind that the investigation should involve *numerical* data (that is, the values of each piece of data are numerical quantities that can be ordered and compared quantitatively, like the family-size data in Olivia's case 3). Your project should also involve comparing at least two groups (e.g., adults and children, men and women, elementary teachers and high school teachers, teachers at one school and teachers at another school).

Designing a Data Investigation

Session Agenda

Sharing homework ("Examples of Student Thinking")	Groups of three Whole group	25 minutes 5 minutes
Case discussion	Groups of three Whole group	20 minutes 15 minutes
Break		**15 minutes**
Math activity ("Surveys of Our Group")	Whole group Groups of four Whole group	25 minutes 30 minutes 10 minutes
Organizing for the data project	Small groups (self-chosen)	30 minutes
Homework and exit cards	Whole group	5 minutes

Background Preparation

Read
- the casebook, chapter 2
- "Maxine's Journal," Session 2 (p. 137)
- the agenda for Session 2

Materials

Prepare
- your responses to participants' first homework papers

Duplicate
- "Focus Questions: Chapter 2" (p. 43)
- class lists
- "Math Activity: Surveys of Our Group" (p. 44)
- "Third Homework" (p. 45)

Obtain
- easel paper and markers
- masking tape (to post charts)
- large index cards or NCR paper (for exit cards)

Agenda

NOTE: Sometime during this class, you may want to help people review one another's names. For example, you could go around the room once with every person saying his or her name, then go around again, saying all the names in unison. Remind participants to similarly review the names of people in their small groups.

Sharing homework   (30 minutes)

Groups of three (25 minutes)

Whole group (5 minutes)

In small groups, participants share their homework writing ("Examples of Student Thinking"). Let them know they have 25 minutes to read and discuss the three papers. Suggest that the people in each group read all three of their papers before they begin any conversation. This way the discussion will include ideas from everyone's paper. They might begin by talking about what surprised them or what they found out about the thinking of their own students. They can also discuss what was the same and what was different among the papers. Each person should have a chance to describe the issues that came up in either their students' thinking or their own thinking about data.

Reserve 5 minutes at the end of this discussion to reflect back one or two ideas that you noticed in their small-group discussions. You may also want to connect issues that you heard in their discussions to issues or questions they raised in their writing for the first (preseminar) homework assignment.

NOTE: If the sharing-homework groups are working well, you may want participants to stay in the same groups for the case discussion.

Case discussion   (35 minutes)

Groups of three (20 minutes)

Whole group (15 minutes)

The cases in chapter 2 explore how a data question is designed to get at certain information about the world. Designing a survey is a common data activity in classrooms. In designing a survey, we have to think through what the purpose of our study is, what questions will get at the information we need, and how the questions might be interpreted by survey participants. In order to find out how questions might be interpreted, we need to pilot and then refine them, based on whether we are obtaining the information that satisfies the purpose of our investigation. As in the first session, focus question 1 urges participants to cite specific evidence for their comments about the cases. While you listen to their conversations, continue to ask participants to point to specific line numbers, to read passages aloud, and to discuss specific students' words or actions.

Reassure participants that in a case discussion, they often will not have time to talk through each question thoroughly, and that you will alert them if there is a question you want all of them to consider so that the whole group can discuss it.

Any of the chapter 2 focus questions can be the basis for whole-group discussion, depending on what comes up in the small groups. You may want to start with a general question about all the cases: How does *purpose* help students in the cases define their questions, determine what data to collect, and interpret their data?

Spend some time on the way the mathematical and emotional issues are intertwined in Sally's episode. Some participants may feel that teachers need to avoid data activities that involve students' feelings. However, most data activities can bring up emotional issues, so it is important to talk about how to deal with these, rather than how to avoid them, by looking specifically at what happened in Sally's case.

Break   (15 minutes)

Math activity: Surveys of our group   (65 minutes)

Whole group (25 minutes)
Groups of four (30 minutes)
Whole group (10 minutes)

This activity has two main parts. First, you lead a brief data collection activity with the whole group. Then, small groups come up with their own question, survey the group, organize, represent, and describe their data. Finally, this work is discussed briefly in the whole group.

Whole-group data collection Lead the group through collecting and representing data, using a line plot, to answer the question *How many years have you been teaching?*

First pose the question and ask participants to think about their answer. Participants are likely to bring up such issues as these: Does student teaching count? What if I taught part of a year? What about substitute teaching? What about college teaching? What if I have another role in the school but I don't teach students? Spend some time talking about how participants might answer these questions and what their rationale would be. This is a chance to make connections to the idea of the *purpose* of a data investigation: What you want to find out helps determine how you would count years of teaching.

Don't let this discussion go on too long. In order to resolve these questions, you can try to get a group consensus, or you can make a choice based on what you would like to know about the group. For example, if you want to know about full-time years of teaching in grades K-6, then you would not count years spent in school in another role. One group decided they wanted to know about full-time responsibility for a classroom, so did not want to count student teaching unless it was a full-year internship.

Sketch a line plot with reasonable intervals (perhaps 5-year intervals) on the board or easel paper. Collect data on the line plot by marking an X for the value of each person's response. Participants saw and discussed a line plot in case 3, and they will see this kind of representation often in this course. Point out that a line plot is a graph for numerical data, similar to a bar graph. It is one of the plots in common use in statistics.

Now, ask the group for statements that describe the data. Help the group focus on the "big picture" of the data. What can they say about the group as a whole in terms of years of teaching? This is a good time to introduce some vocabulary as it comes up in context, such as *range* and (if relevant) *outlier*. See the Data Terms section for further comments on these terms. If ideas about *average* come up, acknowledge them, but let the group know that you'll be spending more time on the idea of average in later sessions.

Help participants list all the statements they can that *describe* the data before moving on to statements of interpretation. Discuss whether there are now ways they would refine the question, or additional questions they would be interested in asking. Point out that in most data activities (including the project they will be doing), they are likely to end up with a clearer idea of the questions they want to ask after they have done some initial data collection and description.

Small-group surveys Ask participants to share some of the possible survey questions they thought of for homework. List these on the board. Then ask the group to give an example of a data value they would get in response to each question. For example, one response to the question *How many hours of sleep do you get?* could be 8 hours. List these examples next to each question, so that you have a list that looks something like this:

How much sleep do you get? 8 hours
How many pairs of sneakers do you own? 3 pairs

Do you use public transportation? yes
Average weekly amount for groceries? $150/week

It is likely that participants will bring up some questions that result in categorical data, such as the question about public transportation, above. If not, generate a couple yourself. Use this list to discuss the difference between numerical and categorical data, referring back to some of the cases they have already read and the data collection they have done in class.

You may find that some confusion about the difference between numerical and categorical data continues over the next couple of sessions. The source of confusion is sometimes the fact that even categorical data involve numbers— that is, we use numbers when we count the frequency of data in a category (7 people use public transportation, 15 people don't). However, even when values and frequency are sorted out, the distinction between the two kinds of data is not always simple. It sometimes helps to ask participants to focus on the nature of each *response* to the question being asked. Is the response a value that can only be put in a category (e.g., *yes, no, red, blue*), or is it a value that can be counted or measured, ordered, and compared (e.g., *52 inches, 6 people in a family*)? See the Data Terms section for a more thorough discussion of this distinction.

Divide the class into groups of four and distribute the math activity handout. Each small group also needs class lists, easel paper, and markers. The groups have about 30 minutes to choose a question that involves numerical data, to survey everyone in the seminar, and to represent and describe the data. As a general guideline for timing, they might spend 15 minutes designing their question and gathering data, then 15 minutes creating a representation on easel paper and writing some statements about what the data show.

Whole-group discussion Once the representations are posted, give everyone a chance to walk around and look at them. The whole-group discussion should focus on what participants learned about the design of their investigations: Did the data they collected help them answer the question they started out with? Do the results suggest ways to refine or revise the question?

Organizing for the data project (30 minutes)

Point out that the group has just collected data about several questions that involved numerical data. Any of these could be refined and pursued for their data investigation. Or they might choose a question from the list they generated earlier in the class, or a question about some issue or problem in their school or community.

Give participants time to form groups that will work on data projects together. You can facilitate the forming of groups in a number of ways. Some participants may be particularly interested in certain questions or topics; ask if anyone already has a question or topic and is looking for other people to work with. Participants from the same school may want to form a group to pursue a topic that is important in their community. Or, groups that worked together today may want to continue work on their question or some new question that came up as they looked at their data.

Groups can contain 2–5 participants, as long as they can find ways to make sure everyone has the opportunity to participate in the work. Since most of the work for this project will be done outside of class, participants who intend to work together should exchange phone and e-mail information.

The first step of this project will be to collect pilot data and present it during Session 4. Piloting their investigation gives participants a chance to try out and refine their question. As you listen to small groups discussing their project, you may need to reiterate the two requirements for this assignment: (1) the project must involve numerical data, and (2) the project must involve the comparison of two groups. The pilot data need not involve two groups unless that is part of what participants need to try out. (For example, if they intend to compare first graders and sixth graders, they might want to make sure that both first graders and sixth graders answer their question in the way it is intended.)

Homework and exit cards

(5 minutes)

Distribute the "Third Homework" handout and index cards or NCR paper for responses to the exit questions. Suggested questions:

1. What case in the casebook has stood out for you, and why?

2. How do you feel about our work together as a group? What is working for you and what isn't?

Before the next session . . .

In preparation for the next session, you need to read and write a response to each participant's portfolio writing—the example of their own students' thinking about a data activity. For more information, see the section in "Maxine's Journal" on responding to the second homework (p. 144).

Be sure to copy each paper and your response for your files before returning them to the participants. In some seminars, participants are interested in having copies of everyone's writing. With their permission, you might duplicate some or all of the assignments so that participants can read one another's work.

Focus Questions: Chapter 2

Cases 4–6

1. In Nadia's case 5, what are the students learning about the relationship between defining the question and the results of their data collection? Point to specific examples to support your ideas about this.

2. Using Sally's case 4, talk through the discussion that starts with Chad's observation that "something's not right" (line 93). What are the students noticing? What are the teacher's and Sally's roles in this conversation? How do Jean Pierre and Eddie participate?

   What important mathematical ideas are coming up in this discussion? What emotional issues are coming up? How are these interconnected?

3. Using Andrea's case 6, think about the connection between the intention or purpose of data collection and how a data investigation is designed.

   a. Consider the first two questions that students came up with in Andrea's class: *How many people in your family?* and *How many houses are on your street?* How could what you want to find out influence how you define each of these questions?

   b. Now review the last part of the episode, about Natasha and Keith (lines 331–362). Natasha seems to have a clear idea of what kind of information she wants. Look carefully at the paragraph about Natasha's ideas about their question. What does she want to find out from this survey? Why do you think she was unhappy about the question they eventually used?

Math Activity: Surveys of Our Group

NOTE: You have 30 minutes to complete this assignment and post a representation of your data for others to see. That means you will need to decide on a question and collect your data efficiently. After 15 minutes, you should be ready to start making a data representation. Your representation need not be elaborate and decorative. Focus on how well it communicates information about your data.

1. Select a question that will result in numerical data.

2. Collect data from everyone in the class.

3. Create a line plot for your data.

4. Write three to five statements on your display that describe your data.

5. When your display is complete, discuss issues that arose in your group as you defined your question.

6. What further questions might you want to pursue, based on these initial data?

Third Homework

Reading assignment: Casebook chapter 3

Read chapter 3 in the casebook for *Working with Data*, including both the introductory text and cases 7–11. Also review Beverly's case 2 in chapter 1, paying attention to how the work in her class is evolving over the year.

Portfolio assignment: Reflections on the seminar

Please respond in writing to these four questions:

1. How is the seminar going for you?

2. What aspect of children's thinking has struck you? What has intrigued or surprised you?

3. What's your current understanding of the difference between *categorical* and *numerical* data? Refer to examples in the cases or in your own work to explain the difference.

4. What questions about data has the seminar raised for you? What are you learning about data? What ideas about data would you like to work on for yourself during the rest of the seminar?

Collecting data for next class

Collect data about your morning commute: How long does it typically take you to get from home to school in the morning? Before our next class, collect data for each day you travel from home to school. Looking at your data, choose a number that you think best represents the amount of time it typically takes you to get from home to school.

Starting the data project

Form a project group of two to five people for your data investigation. Remember that your project needs to involve numerical data and a comparison between two groups (e.g., adults and children, first graders and fourth graders). What is your question? What data do you need? How will you collect them? How will your data provide information about your question? Plan a pilot investigation to try out your question and data collection methods. Your group will present the results of your pilot in Session 4.

Categorical and Numerical Data

Session Agenda

Opening	Whole group	15 minutes
Group norms discussion	Whole group	30 minutes
Case discussion	Groups of three Whole group	30 minutes 15 minutes
Break and logistics		15 minutes
Math activity ("Describing Numerical Data")	Groups of four	40 minutes
Math discussion ("Finding the Median")	Whole group	30 minutes
Homework and exit cards	Whole group	5 minutes

Background Preparation

Read
- the casebook, chapter 3
- "Maxine's Journal," Session 3 (p. 149)
- the agenda for Session 3

Work through
- the math activity, "Describing Numerical Data" (pp. 53–54)

Materials

Prepare
- your responses to participants' second homework, "Examples of Student Thinking"
- a class list, on paper (for photocopying) or on the board, for collecting commute data

Duplicate
- "Case Discussion: Chapter 3" (p. 52)
- class lists (if participants are to copy the commute data from the board)
- "Math Activity: Describing Numerical Data" (pp. 53–54)
- "Fourth Homework" (pp. 55–56)

Obtain
- large index cards or NCR paper (for exit cards)

Agenda

Opening

(15 minutes)

Collect the home-school commute data in such a way that each participant has a list to take home for homework. You might record the information on a single class list and get it photocopied during class if you have duplicating facilities available. Or, put the data on the board for individuals to copy onto class lists you have distributed. In either case, you might list everyone's name on the board before class and have people put their commute time next to their name as they come in.

Take a few minutes for groups to share their plans for their pilot data investigations. At this point in the seminar, some groups may be feeling anxious about the data project. It's important to let participants air their concerns and ask questions they may have. Reassure them that the point of this project is to learn about the *process* of data investigations. At the end of the project, after collecting and analyzing their data, they may feel satisfied that they have useful information, or they may just know more clearly what information they really want and how they would revise their design to get it. Either of these is an acceptable outcome, as long as they can discuss what they learned from doing the project.

Sometimes participants express their concerns by insisting that they need more time during class to work on their project. Explain that in Session 4, there will be time to present and get feedback about their pilot data, but that all other work needs to be done outside of class. You might invite those with further questions to talk with you by phone or by e-mail. Some facilitators have made their seminar meeting room available before or after class for groups to meet about their projects. (See also the ideas under Format and Timing, p. 19.)

Group norms discussion

(30 minutes)

The group norms discussion is a chance for participants to talk about how they're operating together as a group. Since participants have just written a portfolio assignment about how the seminar is going for them, you might begin by asking people to share some of what they wrote about. Encourage them to bring up any concerns about group interactions, about their own learning, and about how to prepare for case discussions. You can also raise any concerns that you have seen on exit cards; for example, how are small-group discussions working?

It's often useful for participants to share what it's like to read cases, why this is a difficult kind of reading, and what they can do to help themselves prepare for class sessions. Some participants have offered comments like these:

"I highlight specific sections that I want to talk about so I can find them easily when I am in class."

"I use the introduction to help me figure out what to look for as I read."

"I write something about each case after I read it—a few sentences that capture what I think it is about."

You might compile some of the suggestions and post them in the meeting room. Further suggestions can be added to the list as the seminar continues.

Case discussion   (45 minutes)

Groups of three (30 minutes)

Whole group (15 minutes)

The cases in chapter 3 present students who are collecting, representing, and interpreting categorical data. At this point in the seminar, participants have worked with categorical data themselves (in Session 1) and have also read cases about students working with categorical data. The case discussion this time involves a group writing assignment that pushes participants to articulate the mathematical ideas with which students are grappling. Participants may find it difficult to be specific about the math ideas, but the very process of trying helps them think more deeply about the students' thinking. Since this approach to the cases differs from the usual focus questions, distribute the "Case Discussion" handout for participants to read before they move into small groups. You might ask someone to paraphrase the group assignment.

Participants may think that half an hour is not enough time to carry out this assignment; you'll need to insist that they concentrate on getting the writing done. One guideline is to spend no more than 10 minutes on each example. At the same time, make sure that each small group works *together* on the writing, rather than each person writing about a different example. The point is to encourage discussion and interaction among participants about the mathematical ideas they see in the cases. Suggest that they consider rotating the responsibility for the writing, because it can be difficult for the writer to participate fully in the discussion. (After mentioning this issue, let groups decide how to handle it, since some people may *not* find it difficult to both write and participate.)

After a half-hour, spend a few minutes having each group briefly share one of their examples. If anyone focuses on Molly's case 11, spend a few minutes on the question it raises, asking, "On what basis would you decide whether *Mummy's Curse* should be included in the data set? Can you think of a situation in which it would be important to include this category and a situation when it would not?"

Collect the examples from each small group and explain that you will duplicate them for distribution in the next session.

Break and logistics
(15 minutes)

At the beginning of break, hand out the homework sheet and (if photocopied) the group's commute-to-school data. Also, ask each data-project group to hand in the question they are investigating and the names of the people in their group. If some groups are still not sure of their question, they should at least give you the list of who is in their group. Use these lists to form discussion groups for sharing pilot data in the next session.

Math activity
(40 minutes)

Form groups of four and distribute the math activity sheet, "Describing Numerical Data." Since participants have been focusing on categorical data in the case discussion, you might reorient them, noting that they are now going to switch back to numerical data. You might also explain that in this activity they are to focus on "getting the big picture" of what a data set shows, and that after they work for a while in small groups, you will come together (in the next activity) to talk about describing the data with one kind of average, the median.

Question 1 on the activity sheet presents a data set that is fairly symmetrical, with the bulk of the data falling in the middle of the range. Question 3 presents a skewed set of data, with most of the data falling in the lower part of the range. Question 2 leads participants to see that omitting values with frequencies of zero gives an incomplete picture of the shape of the data.

Math discussion: Finding the median
(30 minutes)

NOTE: Before gathering the whole group for this discussion, put on the board or easel the two data sets for questions 1 and 3 of the math activity, organized on line plots. Following is the line plot for the data in question 1; see the math activity sheet (p. 54) for the line plot in question 3.

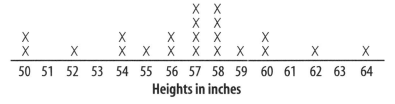

Heights in inches

Call the whole group together and ask for volunteers to briefly describe the two data sets you have posted. In addition, you may want to discuss question 2 from the math activity sheet. When the values with no data are omitted from the line plot, does it make any difference in the overall picture of the data? They might try this with the data set in question 3. Here the shape of the data is clearly very different when values with frequencies of zero are omitted.

Explain that the group is going to start learning about some statistical measures that can be used with numerical data to summarize the data set. First, they'll be focusing on the median; in later sessions, they'll do some work with the mean.

Use the two sets of data on the board to introduce the median. Explain that the median is the value of the middle piece of data in the data set. You might use the analogy of lining up a group of people by height and finding the middle person—that value is the median. Both of these data sets have an odd number of data points, so the median is the value of the middle piece of data. Demonstrate how you would find the median if there were an even number of data points by removing one of the X's on one line plot: The median is then the value midway between the two middle data points. Mention that the median is one form of average, and it is a term they are likely to come across in their daily paper (e.g., the median price of houses in a community).

Ask participants what they can tell about a set of data if they know the extreme values (the lowest and highest) and the median. What do the two halves of the data look like? (Refer back to the two data sets.) Stress the idea that any kind of average provides one piece of information that helps to summarize the data. This is also a good opportunity to look at how little the mode can tell you in a set of numerical data. Modes are useful for categorical data, but with numerical data, a mode may not reveal anything about how the data are spread and where they are clumped. In the height data, the modes happen to be in the center of the data, but in the number-of-years-in-town data, the mode is not helpful. Both median and mean, in different ways, take into account the whole set of data, whereas the mode does not.

Homework and exit cards

Distribute the "Fourth Homework" handout. Call attention to the note that for the next session, project groups are to bring enough copies of their pilot work for everyone in the seminar. Establish how many copies that means, and suggest that each group write that number on their homework handout.

Point out that part of the homework is to look at the group's commute-time data set. They are to represent it, describe it, find the median, and discuss what the median shows about the data. If you have time, participants could begin working on these data now in class in their small groups, then finish the work for homework.

Distribute the exit cards or NCR paper. Suggested questions:

1. What are you learning about collecting, representing, and analyzing data? What are your questions?

2. Was the discussion about how we are working together as a group useful for you?

Before the next session . . .

In preparation for the next session, you need to read and write a response to each participant's portfolio writing, "Reflections on the Seminar." For more information, see the section in "Maxine's Journal" on responding to the third homework (p. 158). Also compile the writing done by all the small groups during this session's casebook discussion, about the children's mathematical ideas they found in chapter 3. Duplicate the complete set for everyone.

Case discussion: Chapter 3

Cases 7–11

The cases in chapter 3 provide examples of students working with categorical data. They are encountering and trying to solve problems about representing categorical data and about choosing categories. Sometimes the students are using knowledge that they have explicitly stated; other times they are acting on ideas that they have not yet articulated or formalized. Part of the hard job of being a classroom teacher is to train your ears and your mind to hear the mathematical ideas being called up by your students.

This assignment is an opportunity to develop and practice that habit in an out-of-classroom setting. In your small group, locate and describe in the cases specific examples of important mathematical ideas students are encountering. Your group should locate examples in at least three different cases.

Explain each example in detail, articulating the mathematical idea, referring to the children's words and actions, and explaining the connection between the mathematical idea and the children's thinking.

As a group, write a paragraph for each example.

- Articulate the mathematical idea that you see.

- Identify the case and the specific passage to which you are referring.

- Explain how the words or actions of the children are related to the math idea.

Each group will share at least one example in the whole-group discussion.

WORKING WITH DATA

Math Activity: Describing Numerical Data

1. Individually or in pairs, sketch a graph of the data in the following table.

Individual	Height (in.)	Individual	Height (in.)
A	57	L	58
B	57	M	58
C	55	N	60
D	54	O	57
E	58	P	52
F	58	Q	56
G	54	R	59
H	60	S	57
I	64	T	62
J	50	U	50
K	56		

Compare your graphs. How would you describe this set of data? As a group, *write down* what you think are the most important statements to make about its shape and spread.

2. Compare the graphs you made with this graph of the same data, made by students in grade 4:

```
                    X   X
                    X   X
   X        X       X   X   X       X
   X   X    X   X   X   X   X   X   X   X   X
   ─────────────────────────────────────────
   50  52  54  55  56  57  58  59  60  62  64
                Heights in inches
```

What are the important differences between these representations? What features of the data are easy to see in each? What features are not easy to see?

WORKING WITH DATA

3. The following graph (from an upcoming case) displays the number of years the families of students in one class, including previous generations, had lived in their town.

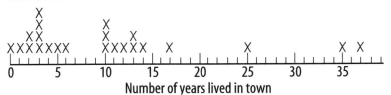

Number of years lived in town

a. Individually, write two or three sentences that you think describe the data well.

b. In your small group, compare your sentences. What does your group think are the most important features of this data set?

WORKING WITH DATA

Fourth Homework

Reading assignment: Casebook chapter 4

Read chapter 4 in the casebook for *Working with Data*, including both the introductory text and cases 12–16.

Portfolio assignment: Pilot for data investigation

Do a pilot test for your data investigation. With your small group, decide how you will test the design of your investigation. For example, if you are doing a survey, try out your survey with a sample of people to see if your survey gives you data that help you answer your question. Are there ways in which you need to modify your questionnaire, or perhaps the way you introduce your questionnaire to respondents? Are there questions you need to add or delete? Are there issues about your target population—which people you will survey—that come up as you do your pilot test?

If you are doing an experiment that involves observation or measurement, test out your observation and measurement techniques. Do they give you useful data? Are there ways in which you need to modify or refine your methods?

For our Session 4 seminar meeting, bring a representation of the data you collected and a few paragraphs that include a description of your data, what you learned from doing the pilot, what questions you now have, and your thoughts about revising your data collection methods. Your group should produce the representation and paragraphs together. That is, this is a *group* assignment, not an individual one. Include everyone's names on the assignment.

NOTE: *Your group should bring enough copies of your work so that every person in the seminar can have a copy.*

Since we will be discussing the pilots in small groups, each member of your group needs to be able to explain what the group did and field questions about your work from others in the seminar.

Math assignment: Representing the commute-to-school data

Make a representation of the group's data on commute time to school. Find the median. Write a few sentences describing the data as if you were reporting on it to someone who didn't have the actual data in front of them. Here are some questions you might want to consider:

- Are there any clumps of data?

- What does the median tell you about the data?

- What can you say about the two halves of the data?

- Are they symmetrically spread around the median or not?

You will be handing in this work at the next session.

Numerical Data: What Do the Numbers Mean?

Session Agenda

Sharing pilot data	Groups of three or four Project groups	30 minutes 30 minutes
Video and small-group case discussion	Whole group (video) Groups of three	10 minutes 35 minutes
Break		**15 minutes**
Whole-group case discussion	Whole group	30 minutes
Math activity ("Median as a Tool . . .")	Groups of three	15 minutes
Homework and exit cards	Whole group	15 minutes

Background Preparation

Read

- the casebook, chapter 4
- "Maxine's Journal," Session 4 (p. 161)
- the agenda for Session 4

Preview

- the video segment for Session 4

Work through

- the math activity, "Median as a Tool in Data Description" (p. 65)

Materials

Prepare

- your responses to participants' third homework, "Reflections on the Seminar"
- four questions for posting (see p. 58)
- copies or overheads of Figures 20, 21, 22, and 24 in case 13 (optional)

Duplicate

- "Focus Questions: Chapter 4" (p. 64)
- "Math Activity: Median as a Tool in Data Description" (p. 65)
- "Lost Teeth Data" (p. 66)
- "Fifth Homework" (p. 67)
- selected curriculum activities for the homework (see list, pp. 62–63)

Obtain

- VCR
- large index cards or NCR paper (for exit cards)

Agenda

Sharing pilot data

(60 minutes)

Groups of three or four (30 minutes)

Project groups (30 minutes)

In this activity, participants get a chance to discuss the progress of their data investigation, get feedback from other participants, and then discuss that feedback and make further plans with their project partners. Post the following questions on the board or easel:

■ What is the question for your data investigation?

■ What did you do for your pilot study?

■ What did you find out?

■ What are your questions?

First, form small groups of three or four, each with representatives from several data project groups. You'll have to form groups according to how many projects there are in the seminar. It's not necessary that every project be represented in every small group. For example, if some are doing the data project in pairs, clearly they can be present in only two small groups. Because of the time involved, it's better not to have more than three projects represented in any one group.

Participants take turns telling about their pilot data and what issues came up for them as they did their pilot investigation. After each participant's report, other group members should give feedback and ask questions. Remind the groups that they have a half-hour, so they need to watch the time and make sure all the group members get to present their work.

For the second half-hour, project groups meet to share the feedback they have received and to make plans for continuing their data project. This is a good time to check in with each group and offer advice.

While everyone in the seminar should receive a copy of the pilot work of every group, some facilitators have noticed that this process can be time-consuming. Note that it's not necessary for everyone to have copies of the projects during the small-group discussion; thus, participants might lay out copies of their pilot work during break for everyone to pick up.

Video and small-group case discussion

Whole group (10 minutes)

Groups of three (35 minutes)

The chapter 4 cases and the video segment—an excerpt from the longer segment shown in Session 1—focus on how students think about the different numbers they encounter as they work with numerical data: both the *value* of each piece of data (e.g., 52 inches, 6 teeth lost, 5 pockets, 3 people in a family), and the *frequency* with which each value occurs (e.g., there are *4 students* who are 52 inches tall, there are *8 third graders* who have lost 6 teeth). Students need to coordinate these two kinds of numbers, always referring back to what the data mean. As participants watch students sort out these ideas, they also have the opportunity to sort out for themselves ideas about the meaning of these numbers that they might never before have considered.

A major portion of this session is devoted to the case discussion. The cases, especially Isabelle's case 13, are complex and raise a number of important issues about numerical data. As a transition into the case discussion, the group views a 4-minute excerpt from the video segment shown in Session 1— the second graders discussing their Pocket Data. Here the students are sorting out value and frequency: which numbers are people and which are pockets? After viewing the video, spend a few minutes on the question, "What mathematical ideas were the students working on?"

With focus questions 1 and 2, small groups should discuss how the students are thinking about the numbers that represent value and frequency in their data. They will also consider how students coordinate these two kinds of numbers in their representations. After about 25 minutes, urge groups to consider focus question 3 and discuss students' ideas about a value of zero in their data.

Break

Whole-group case discussion

In the whole group, focus on Isabelle's case 13 and Denise's case 14. How are students representing the two kinds of numbers they encounter? Focus on the differences between ungrouped data (such as Figure 23 in Isabelle's case, in which each tower shows the value of one piece of data) and data that are grouped by frequency (such as Figures 20 or 21). You will undoubtedly need to spend time discussing Figure 24, in which value and frequency are represented by adjacent pairs of towers.

NOTE: It's useful either to have a separate handout of the figures in case 13 or to put the figures on overheads so that participants don't have to keep flipping pages in the casebook as the discussion progresses.

You may want to briefly address the last part of focus question 3, which asks about the graph in Nadia's case 15, especially if you have noticed confusion or puzzlement in the small groups. The graph shows two variables, one of which is numerical (number of instruments played) and one of which is categorical (whether the person is a girl or boy).

Although there are no focus questions specifically about Maura's case 12, the group worked with the data from this case during the math activity in Session 3. It provides a good example of how a mode can indicate very little about numerical data.

Math activity (15 minutes)

In the math activity, "Median as a Tool in Data Description," participants examine how the median, range, and extremes can be used to summarize and compare data sets. This work will be completed for homework and discussed in the next session. During the short time they have to work on the activity during this session, participants can help each other make sure they understand how to read the data table and how to represent those data in a line plot. A reasonable goal for this 15 minutes would be for every small group to complete a line plot for one of the grade levels. They should bring back the data sheet as well as their completed work on this activity for the next session.

Homework (10 minutes)

For the next portfolio assignment, participants examine specific curriculum materials designed to support children's thinking about the mathematical ideas explored in the seminar. The list on pages 62–63 identifies activities from four different sources; choose two or three of these activities for your seminar group to work with. If you are working in a system that has adopted one of these curricula, your group might work on material only from that curriculum. If your system is in the process of choosing a curriculum, then you might sample two or three sources. If your system has an established curriculum other than these, you might choose relevant activities from that resource.

Since this portfolio assignment is quite different from previous ones, allow extra time at the end of the session for participants to read the "Fifth Homework" handout and ask questions about it. Distribute the two or three activities you have selected. Explain that they will each choose one activity to explore. Emphasize that the most important part of their work will be to determine and articulate the mathematical ideas they would like their students to encounter by working on this activity.

Variation One seminar, presented in a school system that had recently adopted a new curriculum, had a total of 32 participants with at least four from each grade level, K–6. The facilitator selected one activity at each grade, and teachers did the assignment for their grade. When they returned to the seminar, grade-level groups met for 15 minutes to generate a list of ideas that they would want their students to work on through that lesson. Then participants moved to mixed-grade groups for 15 minutes. Starting with kindergarten, teachers briefly explained the lesson that they had examined and shared the top three ideas that their grade-level group had identified. As they went across the grade levels, they discussed how they saw the ideas of data being supported or extended by each lesson shared. Participants explained afterward that this activity gave them a much greater appreciation of their curriculum, having seen how ideas build over the grades.

Data project reminder Remind participants that there will be no further class time for them to work on their group data project and that they should be making arrangements to meet outside of class. All groups will be presenting their projects at the last class session.

Exit cards

(5 minutes)

Distribute the index cards or NCR paper for responses to the exit questions. Suggested questions:

1. How did today's feedback and discussion help your thinking about your data project?

2. Is there something you would like to tell the facilitator about your experience in the seminar?

Before the next session . . .

In preparation for the next session, you need to read and write a response to each project group's report on their pilot investigation. Take into account responses on today's exit cards about what participants learned from the feedback and discussion in this session.

Also respond to participants' representations and descriptions of the commute-to-school data. You may want to write a single group response, highlighting examples from different participants' papers. For more information, see the section in Maxine's Journal on responding to the fourth homework (p. 166). Remember to copy both the papers and your responses for your files before returning the work.

Summary

Working with Data

Pocket Data (excerpt), 4 minutes

This segment is excerpted from the video you showed in Session 1. The segment begins when the teacher draws her second graders' attention to the completed line plot by asking what they notice about the data.

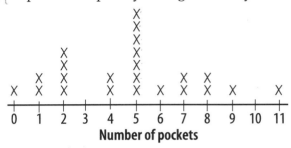

Number of pockets

When Denise says, "I noticed that 5 has a lot," the teacher asks, "If 5 has a lot, what does that tell us about our group?" In the conversation that follows, students try to articulate what the statement tells about the class. They struggle with sorting out what the numbers along the bottom of the plot mean (the values) and what the number of X's above each value means (the frequency with which each value occurs).

Curriculum Resources

Choose two or three activities from this list for seminar participants to explore as homework for discussion in Session 5. Duplicate all relevant material from the teacher's guides and any student material required.

Everyday Mathematics (Chicago: Everyday Learning Corporation, 2001)

LEVEL/BOOK:	*Second Grade Everyday Mathematics*
ACTIVITY:	"Data Day: Standing Jumps and Arm Spans," "Middle Value (Median) of a Set of Data," and "Frequency Distributions" (Lessons 7.7, 7.8, and 7.9)
DUPLICATE:	Second Grade Teacher's Lesson Guide, Vol. 2, pp. 545–549, 550–553, and 556–560 Second Grade Math Masters, pp. 22, 134, and 337–338 Second Grade Math Journal 2, pp. 178–179 and 184–185

LEVEL/BOOK:	*Fifth Grade Everyday Mathematics*
ACTIVITY:	"Organizing Data" (Lesson 6.1)
DUPLICATE:	Fifth Grade Teacher's Lesson Guide, Vol. 1, pp. 350–353
	Fifth Grade Math Masters: p. 282
	Fifth Grade Math Journal 1, pp. 170–171

Investigations in Number, Data, and Space (Glenview, IL: Scott Foresman)

LEVEL/BOOK:	Grade 1, *Survey Questions and Secret Rules* (Collecting and Sorting Data) by T. Wright and J. Mokros, 1998
ACTIVITY:	"Would You Rather Be an Eagle or a Whale?"
DUPLICATE:	Investigation 2, Sessions 1 and 2, pp. 34–42
	Student Sheet 4, p. 115

LEVEL/BOOK:	Grade 4, *The Shape of the Data* (Statistics) by S. J. Russell, R. B. Corwin, A. Rubin, and J. Akers, 1998
ACTIVITY:	"How Many People in a Family?"
DUPLICATE:	Investigation 1, Sessions 2 and 3, pp. 13–19
	Student Sheet 1, p. 73

MathLand: Journeys Through Mathematics (Mountain View, CA: Creative Publications)

LEVEL/BOOK:	*Grade 3 Guidebook*, by L. Charles et al., 1995
ACTIVITY:	"Getting to Know You"
DUPLICATE:	pp. 224–227

LEVEL/BOOK:	*Grade 5 Guidebook*, by L. Charles et al., 1995
ACTIVITY:	"Comparison Polls"
DUPLICATE:	pp. 176–179

Math Trailblazers (Dubuque, IA, Kendall/Hunt, 1998)

LEVEL/BOOK:	Grade 2
ACTIVITY:	"Marshmallows and Containers" (Unit 6, Lesson 5)
DUPLICATE:	Unit Resource Guide, pp. 219–224
	Student Guide, pp. 65–69
	Discovery Assignment Book, p. 82

LEVEL/BOOK:	Grade 5
ACTIVITY:	"Life Spans" (Unit 8, Lesson 5)
DUPLICATE:	Unit Resource Guide, pp. 791–800
	Student Guide, pp. 141, 277–279

Focus Questions: Chapter 4

Cases 12–16

1. In Isabelle's case 13, look carefully at the pictured work of the four groups listed below and reread the discussions of their work. (Keep in mind that Isabelle's class had collected data from four different classrooms, and each group is working with only one classroom's data. Therefore, different displays do not necessarily represent the same data.)

   Figure 20. Seth, Tracy, and Nikolai (lines 202–266)

   Figure 22. Lamont, Franklin, and Karyn (lines 279–289)

   Figure 23. Peter, Kevin, Gabrielle, and Eddy (lines 290–296 and 365–428)

   Figure 24. Neil and Morgan (lines 297–309 and 317–359)

   How does each group show the number of people and the number of teeth? How does each group coordinate these two numbers?

2. In Denise's case 14, how is Kenny representing the data? How are Cara and Tim representing the data? What is the meaning of an X in Kenny's graph? What is the meaning of an X in Cara's and Tim's graphs? Why do you think they are having a difficult time understanding each other's representations?

3. In Nadia's class (case 15), an issue is raised about a value of zero. What is Rico's argument (line 488) about why the value of 0 *should not* be on the graph? What are James's and Nicole's arguments (lines 498–504) about why 0 *should* be shown on the graph?

   On what basis would you decide whether a value of 0 should be included in the data? Try to think of an example of a data set in which you *would* include zero and an example in which you would not.

   Also in Nadia's case, what kind of data are represented on the graph in Figure 27 (p. 85)? Are they categorical or numerical?

4. Given all that you have noticed about how students in grades 2–5 describe numerical data, look at Barbara's case 16. In what ways are these kindergarten students beginning to consider important ideas about numerical data?

Math Activity: Median as a Tool in Data Description

1. Refer to the table on the "Lost Teeth Data" handout as you represent the data for each grade, K–3, on a line plot. (You will see students working with these same data on a videotape in the next session.)

2. Describe and compare the four sets of data. Are the four grades similar? Different?

3. If just the mode for each grade were reported to you, what would that tell you about the data? What wouldn't you be able to tell?

4. Find the median number of teeth lost for each grade. If just the median for each grade were reported to you, how would that help you compare the grade levels?

5. If just the median and the range were reported to you, what could you say about the data? If just the lowest value, the highest value, and the median for each grade were reported, what could you say about the data? Would these statistics give you an adequate picture of the data? What would you know about the data? What wouldn't you know?

Lost Teeth Data

Lost Teeth, Grades K–3

Number of teeth lost	Number of students			
	Kindergarten	Grade 1	Grade 2	Grade 3
0	10	2		
1	1	0		
2	2	2	1	1
3	2	2		
4	1	2		
5	0	2		2
6	1	1		1
7		4	2	
8		1	8	4
9		1	3	5
10		2	2	2
11		0	1	
12		1	2	1
13			1	2
14				1
15				
16				1
17				
18				
19				1
Don't know				2

Fifth Homework

Reading assignment: Casebook chapter 5

Read chapter 5 in the casebook for *Working with Data*, including both the introductory text and cases 17–19.

Portfolio assignment: Examining curriculum materials

In this assignment, you will examine a set of curriculum materials to determine which mathematical ideas it could raise for your students and to consider how you might highlight those ideas. Read over the materials and choose *one* activity to focus on. You should not feel limited by the particulars of the lesson, such as grade level. By focusing on its mathematical potential, consider how you could use this material as a basis for work with your own students, with grade-level adaptations as needed. Once you are familiar with the material, consider these questions:

1. When using this activity, what mathematical ideas would you want your students to work through?

2. How would you work to bring that mathematics out?

3. How would you modify the lesson to make it more accessible or more challenging for your students?

4. What questions might you ask them as you watch them work?

5. What might you learn about their understanding by listening to them or by observing them?

NOTE: You might be tempted to do this lesson with your students as part of this work—but please don't do this before the next class. At our next session, you'll have a chance to share ideas with others in the seminar who worked on the same curriculum activity. If you do want to try this material with your students, wait until after that conversation.

REMINDER: *Bring four copies of your writing to the next session.*

Math assignment: Lost teeth data

Finish working on the math activity we began in class ("Median as a Tool in Data Description") and be ready to discuss your work at the next session.

5

WORKING WITH DATA

Comparing Data Sets

Session Agenda

Sharing homework (curriculum materials)	Groups of three	20–30 minutes
Math activity (Lost Teeth homework and "Stem-and-Leaf Plots")	Whole group Groups of four	30 minutes 35 minutes
Break		15 minutes
Math discussion ("Stem-and-Leaf Plots")	Whole group	10 minutes
Video viewing and discussion	Whole group	20 minutes
Case discussion	Groups of three Whole group	20–30 minutes 15 minutes
Homework and exit cards	Whole group	5 minutes

Background Preparation

Read
- the casebook, chapter 5
- "Maxine's Journal," Session 5 (p. 172)
- the agenda for Session 5
- the section on stem-and-leaf plots in "Data Terms: A Glossary" (p. 116)

Work through
- the math activity, "Stem-and-Leaf Plots" (pp. 77–79)

Preview
- the video segment for Session 5

Materials

Prepare
- your responses to the commute-to-school data homework and to each project group's report on their pilot data
- an unordered list of the group's commute data (from Session 3), on the board or easel paper

Duplicate
- "Math Activity: Stem-and-Leaf Plots" (pp. 77–79)
- "Lost Teeth Bar Graph" (p. 80)
- "Focus Questions: Chapter 5" (p. 81)
- "Sixth Homework" (p. 82)

Obtain
- VCR
- large index cards or NCR paper (for exit cards)

SESSION 5

Agenda

Sharing homework (curriculum materials) (20–30 minutes)

NOTE: If you are using the variation for the review of curriculum materials (as suggested on p. 61), explain that participants will first meet in grade-level groups, then in mixed-grade groups, in order to trace the development of ideas across the grades. The variation will take 30 minutes (15 minutes each in grade-level and mixed-grade groups). If you are using the standard format described below, you will need about 20 minutes for this activity, which gives you an extra 10 minutes for the video and case discussion.

Sort the participants into groups according to the curriculum activity they chose to review. After this sorting, subdivide each larger group into groups of three or four. Remind participants to read the other two or three papers for their small group before beginning any discussion.

One facilitator noted that some participants weren't sure what "counts" as a mathematical idea. This facilitator first spent a few minutes with the whole group, asking for examples of mathematical ideas about working with data that they'd noticed in the cases. Once having heard some ideas from one another, it was easier for participants to move into the small-group discussions.

As you listen in on small groups, help participants articulate the set of mathematical ideas they expect their students to work on by using these materials. To refocus a discussion that is veering off the topic, try paraphrasing the questions on the homework handout: What mathematics will students encounter by doing this? What questions might you ask while they work? What would you expect to learn about their thinking by asking that?

NOTE: For the next portfolio assignment, participants are to write a case based on data work in their own classroom. Some groups may want to work with the curriculum materials they have reviewed so they can share lesson plans and outcomes with one another. If this is the case, plan to group these people together in the next session when participants share their write-ups.

Math activity

Whole group (30 minutes)

Groups of four (35 minutes)

Sharing the "Lost Teeth" homework Start with a brief whole-group discussion of the math activity that participants completed for homework, working with the Lost Teeth data. Focus on what the median tells you about the data: How does the median help you compare the four groups? This is a good time to check whether anyone still has questions about how to find the median. Participants are likely to ask how to treat "don't know" responses when finding the median. Since these are categorical, not numerical, values, they can't be ordered with the rest of the data, and so can't be counted in finding the median. They could be reported separately, perhaps as a percentage of the responses.

An important idea to cover in this discussion is that the median, by itself, only provides the middle value in the data set—that is, we know that half the values are equal to or below the median, and half the values are equal to or above the median value. However, without any other information, we can't tell anything about how the data are spread around the median: for example, are most of the data clustered around the median value, or are they very spread out?

Stem-and-leaf plots Explain that today and in the next session, you are going to introduce two kinds of representations that may be unfamiliar to this group: stem-and-leaf plots (today) and box plots (next session). These are not representations the teachers will use with their students (unless some are middle school teachers), but are a type of display they might choose to use in their own data projects for this seminar. Stem-and-leaf and box plots can also help the participants think in new ways about describing data (in terms of shape, spread, and center), about the use of the median, and about how to compare two or more data sets (see "Why Stem-and-Leaf and Box Plots?" on p. 71).

Explain briefly that these are relatively new representations in the history of statistics, having been introduced (along with the line plot) in the 1960s and 1970s. They are commonly used by statisticians and appear in many middle school and high school curriculum materials. Both types of plot are discussed in the Data Terms section (see pp. 116–118).

Demonstrate how to make a stem-and-leaf plot, using the group's commute-to-school data. The stem should show the tens digit for the number of minutes traveled and the leaves should show the ones digit. Work slowly, making sure everyone can read the data values. It often helps to point out that this plot is like a bar graph turned ninety degrees, with the bars horizontal instead of vertical. Following is an example of the commute-to-school data from one seminar:

```
0 | 5 5 9
1 | 1 5 6 6 7
2 | 0 0 0
3 | 4 5 5 5 5
4 | 5 5
5 | 0
6 |
7 | 5
```

3 | 5 is 35 minutes

Once you think most participants can read the plot, ask them what they can say about the shape and spread of the data. With the class, find the median. People new to this kind of plot often need reminders to consider the data *in order* as they find the median. In other words, if they are counting up from the lowest value (5) to find the tenth piece of data, they need to remember to move from the end of the ones line (9) to the *beginning* of the tens line (11), not to the end of the tens line (17).

Why Stem-and-Leaf and Box Plots?

Learning about new tools for representing and analyzing data is one way teachers learn about data in this seminar. There are several reasons for teaching elementary teachers about representational and statistical tools (such as the arithmetic mean or box plots) that they will not use directly with their students.

First, many teachers have never encountered statistical tools beyond those commonly seen in the popular media, which include bar graphs, pie charts, an occasional line graph, and some mentions of *average*. Learning about other tools helps them expand their own knowledge of the wide range of statistical tools in use today and may help them see that statistics is a living and growing field in which new tools and representations are being developed to meet new needs.

Second, the particular tools introduced in this course are now commonly integrated into middle and high school statistics work because they offer useful and accessible representations for representing, describing, and comparing data sets. Stem plots provide a way to compare the center and spread of two data sets; box plots offer compact summaries of large data sets and provide a means to compare several groups.

Becoming familiar with these representations develops teachers' skills in summarizing data and helps them move away from the bar graph as an all-purpose tool. As they consider how different representations provide different views of the data, they can better help students develop and evaluate their own representations.

Next, demonstrate construction of a stem-and-leaf plot for the height data from a fourth-grade class, shown below as Phoebe's class. First use just 5 and 6 in the stem, as shown here.

Student heights in Phoebe's class

```
5 | 0 0 2 4 4 5 6 6 7 7 7 7 8 8 8 8 9
6 | 0 0 2 4
                        5 | 2 is 52 inches
```

Then, show how to break each decade into two parts (50 to 54 inches, 55 to 59 inches, 60 to 64 inches) to demonstrate that we can select intervals that best show something about the data.

Student heights in Phoebe's class

```
5 | 0 0 2 4 4
• | 5 6 6 7 7 7 7 8 8 8 8 9
6 | 0 0 2 4
            5 | 2 is 52 inches
```

Mention that with another set of data, the stem might not represent tens, but might represent hundreds or millions or tenths. That is why a stem-and-leaf plot needs a key to indicate what the values in the stem and the leaves are.

Finally, show how this plot could be made into a back-to-back stem-and-leaf plot by adding another set of data for Marion's class, as shown.

Student heights

Marion's class			Phoebe's class
4 4 4 4 3 3 3 2 1 1 1 0 0	5		0 0 2 4 4
8 6 6 5 5	•		5 6 6 7 7 7 7 8 8 8 8 9
1 0	6		0 0 2 4
5	•		

```
                    | 5 | 2 is 52 inches
```

Briefly, ask the class to use the stem-and-leaf plot to compare the heights of the two classes.

Distribute the math activity handout with stem-and-leaf plots 1 and 2. Participants work on the questions in small groups. Sometimes they become very involved in the jump-rope data (question 1b). You'll need to make sure they get to question 2 with at least 20 minutes left before break. Be prepared to hand out the Lost Teeth bar graph (p. 80) as groups request a copy, *after* completing their back-to-back stem-and-leaf plot.

Break

Math discussion (stem-and-leaf plots)

If you have time for a whole-group discussion, ask participants to compare the stem-and-leaf plots to the bar graph. If you don't have time now, consider starting with this at the beginning of the next session's math work.

In either case, emphasize that participants will need to bring their work and handouts from this session for reference in the next session's math activity.

Video viewing and discussion   (20 minutes)

The video and cases for this session focus on comparing data sets, using ideas about the shape, spread, and center of the data. Although we often use single data sets for instructional purposes in elementary classrooms, comparison is commonly what we use statistics for.

Tell participants that they'll be viewing the video of the class that collected the Lost Teeth data they've been working with. Watch the video in segments, with brief discussions between the segments. However, keep in mind that the complete video is a little over 14 minutes long, so your total discussion time is only about 5 minutes. Participants can continue referring to the video during their small-group case discussion.

Before the first segment, ask participants to notice the ideas students on the video offer about any differences there are between the grades. Stop after this segment to briefly discuss this. Also ask, "Why do you think the teacher chose to ask them about how the range might change for different grades?"

Then show the next segment (the students who report about the first-grade data). Ask, "Did the children notice what you consider to be important features of the data? Are there features they didn't notice?"

Consider the same questions after showing the final segment (students reporting on the kindergarten and third-grade data), either as a whole group or in the following small-group case discussion.

Variation This is a very packed session. If time is running short, some facilitators show the video, then ask participants to begin their small-group case discussion by talking about the video. In this case, it is important to post questions about the video before participants view it. Ask them to take notes on the video for discussion in their small groups.

Case discussion

Groups of three (20–30 minutes)

Whole group (15 minutes)

In small groups, participants finish their discussion of the video and then turn to the cases, discussing the focus questions for chapter 5. They should concentrate on questions 1 and 2, then move on to question 3 as time allows. If you have time for some whole-group discussion, you can choose threads from the small-group discussion that you think everyone should hear, or ask the group what they noticed about the role of comparison in students' thinking in these cases.

Homework and exit cards
(5 minutes)

In preparation for next session's case discussion, say something to the group about reading the cases carefully and taking notes to prepare for the discussion. Because the cases raise a number of complex issues about students' ideas about average, the group will spend a long time in case discussion. Explain that the session will go better for everyone if they are diligent in their preparation and come to class having worked through the students' thinking carefully, with notes on what strikes them as important. Point out that they will also be thinking through their own ideas about average as they try to understand the students' ideas.

Distribute the index cards or NCR paper for responses to the exit questions. Suggested questions:

1. What are your understandings or confusions about the median? *Or:* What did you learn from working with the stem-and-leaf plots?

2. What did you get out of doing the curriculum review assignment?

NOTE: Remind participants they will need the Lost Teeth data from their Session 4 homework for use in the next session. Have extra copies on hand (p. 66) in case some participants forget to bring the data to class.

Before the next session . . .

In preparation for the next session, read the papers that teachers wrote while doing their curriculum review and prepare a summary that represents the ideas of all the papers. For more information, see the section in "Maxine's Journal" on responding to the fifth homework (p. 183).

Video Summary

Working with Data

How Many Teeth Have We Lost? 14 minutes 30 seconds

This second-grade class is investigating the question, *How many teeth have we lost?* They have previously collected data from their own class and from other classes in the school. The video, set up for viewing in three segments, shows the group discussing and representing their data.

Segment 1

The teacher holds a brief discussion before they graph the data from the other classes. She asks, "What kind of ranges do you think we might find in some of the other grades?" Some students actually remember from their data collection what the maximum and minimum values are. Others make predictions based on their own experience and reasoning.

One student mentions that there can be variability in kindergarten—that some students might lose teeth early, even though they are young. The teacher asks, "How would that affect the range?" The student makes the argument that the range might be a little higher than they might expect because of this variability.

Another student seems to agree. He recounts his own experience losing a tooth when he was young. He points out that there is a lot of variability in their own class—he speculates that different bodies are different.

Segment 2

After their initial discussion, the second graders worked in pairs and small groups to graph data from the other classes. The next segment of this video begins as two girls share their graph of the first-grade data. They report the total number of teeth lost and the mode.

The girls point out a clump of data in the lower numbers, at 2–5. The teacher asks for someone else to explain this idea in their own words. Kurt says that the data are "all squooshed together" at 2 through 5. The teacher asks where the clump was for their own class; students reply that it was at 8 and 9.

One of the girls anounces her surprise that any first graders had lost 12 teeth and speculates that they may have had teeth pulled out by the dentist.

This segment opens toward the end of the presentation by students who graphed the third-grade data. The class has noticed that this graph includes a category of students who didn't know how many teeth they had lost. The teacher asks why that might be. Jimmy responds that maybe they lost some of the teeth a long time ago and can't remember. Another student adds that perhaps they have lost so many teeth that it's difficult to keep track of the number.

Finally, Rebecca and Jamie share their data from a kindergarten class. They report that the data ranged from 0 to 6 and that 10 of the students had not lost any teeth, but not many had lost 3 or 4 or 5 or 6. Jamie says they were surprised that one student had lost 6 teeth because that is very close to some students in their own class who had lost 7 teeth. The class identifies a clump of data at 0–2.

WORKING WITH DATA

Math Activity: Stem-and-Leaf Plots

1. Examine the two examples of stem-and-leaf plots on the next two sheets.

   a. What do the numbers mean on each plot?

   b. How would you compare the two classes in the jump-rope activity?

2. Split your group into pairs. Each pair should do the following:

   Create a back-to-back stem-and-leaf plot to compare the Lost Teeth data for grades 1 and 3. You will need to decide whether the stem should go by tens or some other interval. (Refer to your Session 4 homework for these data.)

   When both pairs in your group have finished, come back together and compare the stem-and-leaf plots you've created. Ask the facilitator for a bar graph of the same data, and compare your stem-and-leaf plots to this bar graph. What does each type of representation help you see about the data? Are some features of the data easier to notice on one or the other?

Stem-and-leaf plot 1

Consider this jump-rope data collected from two school classes. Which class did better overall?

Numbers of Jumps

Ms. R's Class		Mr. K's Class
8 7 7 7 5 1 1	0	1 1 2 3 4 5 8 8
6 1 1	1	0 7
9 7 6 3 0 0	2	3 7 8
5 3	3	0 3 5
5 0	4	2 7 8
	5	0 2 3
2	6	0 8
	7	
9 8 0	8	
6 3 1	9	
	10	2 4
3	11	
	12	
	13	
	14	
	15	1
	16	0 0
	17	
	18	
	19	
	20	
	21	
	22	
	23	
	24	
	25	
	26	
	27	
	28	
	29	
	30	0

7|3|0 means 37 jumps for Ms. R's class and 30 jumps for Mr. K's class

SOURCE: *Data About Us,* Teacher's Edition, by G. Lappan, J. T. Fey, W. M. Fitzgerald, S. N. Friel, & E. D. Phillips (Upper Saddle River, NJ: Prentice Hall, 2002), p. 107.

SESSION 5

WORKING WITH DATA

Stem-and-leaf plot 2

This plot records the number of home runs hit by the top home-run hitter in each league for the years 1921 through 2001. For example, Hack Wilson (Chicago) led the National League in home runs in 1926, hitting 21. His is the lowest value shown. The two highest values, 70 and 73, represent the number of home runs hit by Mark McGwire (St. Louis) in 1998 and Barry Bonds (San Francisco) in 2001. Until 1998, the American League held the record, set by Roger Maris (New York) with 61 home runs in 1961, just barely beating Babe Ruth's (New York) long-held record of 60 home runs, set in 1927. Since data on a stem-and-leaf plot are ordered by value, you can't tell from this plot which value occurred in which year.

Home-Run Leaders, 1921–2001

National League		American League
1	2	
3 3	•	2 2
	•	4
7	•	
9 8 8 8	•	
1 1 1 1 0 0	3	
3 3	•	2 2 2 2 2 2 2 3 3
5 5 4 4	•	4 5
7 7 7 7 6 6 6 6	•	6 6 6 6 7 7 7 7
9 9 9 8 8 8 8	•	9 9 9 9 9
1 1 0 0 0 0 0 0	4	0 0 0 0 1 1 1
3 3 3 3 2 2	•	2 2 2 2 3 3 3 3
5 5 4 4 4 4	•	4 4 4 4 4 5 5
7 7 7 7 7 7 6 6 6	•	6 6 6 6 6 6 7 7
9 9 9 9 8 8 8	•	8 8 8 9 9 9 9 9 9
1 1 0	5	0 1
2 2	•	2 2 2
4	•	4
6	•	6 6
	•	8 8 9
	6	0 1
	•	
5	•	
	•	
	•	
0	7	
3	•	

9 | 3 | represents 39 home runs

SOURCE: Home-run data for 1921–93 are from *Exploring Data,* Teacher's Edition, by J. M. Landwehr & A. E. Watkins (Parsippany, NJ: Dale Seymour, 1996), p. 36. Data for 1994–2001 are from MLB.com, The Official Site of Major League Baseball. Retrieved October 8, 2001, from http://www.mlb.com

Lost Teeth Bar Graph

The graph below is a representation of some of the student data recorded in the table "Lost Teeth, Grades K–3," which was distributed in Session 4.

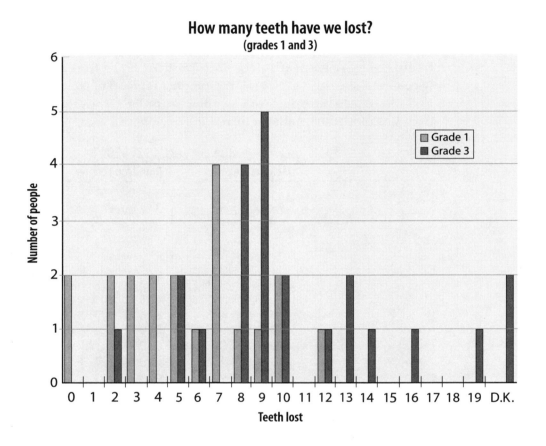

How many teeth have we lost?
(grades 1 and 3)

Focus Questions: Chapter 5

Cases 17–19

1. In Evelyn's case 17, look at two student conversations.

   a. In the conversation (lines 15–19) that occurs when students first look at their own data, how are they interpreting the graph? What do they understand about their data and how the data are represented?

   b. When students look at the kindergarten and first-grade data (lines 54–60), how does their discussion differ from the first discussion? Why do you think the conversation is different now?

   c. Evelyn thinks that "Making comparisons between the two graphs really helped them understand the data better" (line 63). Do you agree? Why or why not?

2. Georgia (case 19) has struggled all year with what is important for her third graders to think about when they describe and interpret data.

   a. In her case, find student statements that you think indicate something important about comparing these sets of data. What does each student notice, and why is it important?

   b. At the end of case 19, Georgia speculates about the role of comparison in helping students make sense of the data. Read over the questions she poses in lines 377–383. What do you think about the issues she brings up? Point to specific examples in the case that illustrate your ideas.

3. Josie's case 18 shows a fourth-grade class investigating sleep. For *each* group of students in this case:

   a. Analyze the results yourself. How would you compare the different grade levels? Describe how they are similar or different, as reflected in the data.

   b. Think about how the students formulated their question and collected their data, how they represented their data, and how they analyzed their data. How did the fact that students were comparing results for different grade levels affect their work?

Sixth Homework

Reading assignment: Casebook chapter 6

Read chapter 6 in the casebook for *Working with Data*, including both the introductory text and cases 20–24.

Portfolio assignment: Students' thinking about comparing groups

Write about a data experience with your students in which they compare two groups (e.g., two different grades, two different classes, children and adults). Recount what the students said and did, using as much detail as you can. As you consider your students' thinking, write about what stood out for you, what confused you, what surprised you, what your questions are. As a part of your writing, consider this question: How are your students making sense of the "big picture" of the data?

REMINDER: *Bring three copies of your writing to the next session.*

Math assignment: Data project

Continue working with your partners on your data project.

6

Average: Developing Ideas about 'Middle'

Session Agenda

Sharing written homework	Groups of three	30 minutes
	Whole group	5 minutes
Small-group case discussion	Groups of three	60 minutes
Break		**15 minutes**
Whole-group case discussion	Whole group	20 minutes
Math activity ("Box Plots")	Whole group	15 minutes
	Groups of four	30 minutes
Homework and exit cards	Whole group	5 minutes

Background Preparation

Read
- the casebook, chapter 6
- "Maxine's Journal," Session 6 (p. 184)
- the agenda for Session 6
- the section on Box Plots in "Data Terms: A Glossary" (pp. 117–118)

Work through
- the math activity, "Box Plots" (pp. 89–90)

Materials

Prepare
- your summary of the ideas in participants' fifth homework, "Examining Curriculum Materials"
- an ordered list of the group's commute data (from Session 3), on the board or easel

Duplicate
- "Focus Questions: Chapter 6" (p. 88)
- "Math Activity: Box Plots" (pp. 89–90)
- "Lost Teeth Data" (p. 66), extra copies for participants who forget theirs
- "Seventh Homework" (p. 91)
- "Averages, Part 1" (p. 92)
- "Displaying Data" (p. 93)

Obtain
- large index cards or NCR paper (for exit cards)

Agenda

Sharing written homework

Groups of three (30 minutes)

Whole group (5 minutes)

Assign participants to groups of three to read and discuss their portfolio writing: classroom "cases" looking at their own students' thinking about using data to compare groups. Consider grouping by grade level so that teachers at the same or similar grade levels can get a sense of what is possible as they listen to their colleagues. Groups have about 10 minutes to spend discussing each person's writing; remind them to watch the time so that everyone gets a chance to share.

It's probably best for the group to read and discuss one paper at a time, since reading three cases all at once is a lot to take in. Here are two guiding questions for the discussions that you might put on the board:

■ What did you learn about your own students' understandings about using data to compare groups?

■ What do you notice by examining the collection of cases from your group?

As a transition to the case discussion, pull the whole group together and ask them to briefly share what they noticed about their students' work with comparing two groups.

Small-group case discussion

Participants have begun to think about and use averages as they've learned about median in the last few seminar sessions. Now they will delve more deeply into students' ideas about averages, how these ideas develop from everyday notions of "average," and how they come to understand the nature and uses of the statistical measures called *averages*.

Distribute the focus questions for chapter 6. Point out that small groups will have an hour to work through these questions and that they should spend some time on each one. Question 1 asks them to compare the ways *average* is used in everyday language and in mathematics. The remaining questions ask them to think about the ideas of "most" and "middle" that students encounter as they try to summarize data or to describe what is typical about a group. You may need to be more vigilant than usual about moving groups along so that they spend some time on each of the four questions.

Break
(15 minutes)

Whole-group case discussion
(20 minutes)

Use these questions to focus the whole-group discussion:

- What are examples of students' "everyday ideas" about average?

- What examples of students' mathematical ideas about average did you find in the cases?

- What are your ideas about what an average is?

- What does an average tell you about the data it represents?

- What different kinds of "middles" come up in the students' work? What does each of these middles show about the data?

During this discussion, you may want to clarify that both the *median* and the *mean* are averages. Participants may have questions about the mean, and you can point out that they will be doing some work with the mean in the next session.

Math activity
(45 minutes)

Whole group (15 minutes)
Groups of four (30 minutes)

This math activity continues the work of learning about new data representations. It also extends participants' work with median as they learn to divide the data into four equal parts to construct a box plot.

To introduce this activity, tell participants that the box plot (sometimes called box-and-whiskers) is a representation that *summarizes* the data, using the median and quartiles. Essentially, a box plot divides the data into quarters to give a view of how the data are spread across the range. Box plots are useful with large data sets and are particularly useful for comparing groups.

Using your group's commute-to-school data, demonstrate how to construct a box plot. First draw the scale (a line showing the full range of the data). Looking at the ordered data, locate the median, then the lower and upper quartiles.

Draw a box above the scale, showing the middle 50 percent of the data. Then draw lines connecting the box to points at the lower and upper extremes. Following is an example using teachers' commute data collected during one seminar. (This is the same data represented in a stem-and-leaf plot on p. 71).

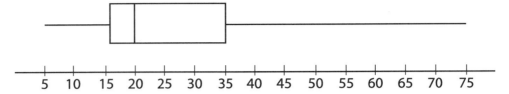

Ask participants what they can see about the data from this representation. Are the data spread evenly across all four quartiles or are they concentrated? How does looking at the middle 50 percent of the data help us understand the data set as a whole?

In the example above, the box plot shows that the data ranged from 5 to 75 minutes commute time. The median is at 20. What is particularly striking in this representation is that the lower half of the data is much more compressed than the upper half of the data. The middle 50 percent of the data goes from 15.5 to 35 minutes, but a quarter of the data are concentrated between 15.5 and 20 minutes.

You may want to mention the variation of using asterisks to mark outliers. In this case, if we considered the single value at 75 minutes as an outlier, the right whisker would reach only to 50. While the upper half of the data would still be more spread out, the spread is not as dramatic as when we use 75 as the endpoint for the whisker. Even so, about half the teachers have commute times within a 15-minute range (from 5 to 20 minutes), while the other half have commute times more than twice that range (from 20 to 50 minutes).

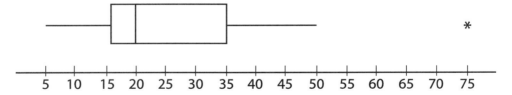

Distribute the math activity sheet with the two examples of box plots. Participants work on this sheet in small groups for the rest of the session. Make sure that every group moves on to question 2 with enough time to construct the two box plots for themselves.

If participants finish their box plots, you might end the session by having the whole group look at and describe them. How do they summarize the data? What does the box plot show? How does the box plot differ from a stem-and-leaf plot or bar graph?

Homework and exit cards

Distribute the "Seventh Homework" handout and "Averages, Part 1," which participants will complete for homework. Also hand out the reference sheet, "Displaying Data," and suggest that participants read through it before the next class. Encourage them to bring back any questions about the new plots and their uses.

Be sure participants recognize that the reading for the next class is *not* the cases in chapter 7, but the "Highlights of Related Research" essay in chapter 8. The reasoning behind discussing the research essay in Session 7 is that the research essay is more dense than the cases, and you want to make sure that all participants devote enough time to reading the essay. Since their data projects are due at the last session, it does not work well to have a heavy reading assignment for that session as well. The chapter 7 cases will be discussed in Session 8. You might suggest that participants plan to read the research essay in two or three sittings.

Hand out index cards or NCR paper for responses to the exit questions:

1. What are you learning about students' thinking about averages?

2. Comment on your own understanding about average, especially median.

Before the next session . . .

In preparation for the next session, read and write responses to the papers that teachers wrote about their students' thinking in using data to compare groups. For more information, see the section in "Maxine's Journal" on responding to the sixth homework (p. 193). Copy both the papers and your responses for your files before returning the work. If you think your participants would benefit from reading all the papers, make copies of the complete set for your group.

Focus Questions: Chapter 6

Cases 20–24

1. What are the different ideas about average brought up by the students in Isabelle's case 20 and Lucy's case 21? List the students' different definitions of *average* and identify which students are talking about each of these ideas. Which of these refer to the way *average* is used in everyday language? Which refer to the way *average* is used in mathematics?

2. In Lucy's case 21, students are developing some ideas about an average value.

   a. What ideas about average come up as they consider their height data? as they analyze the button data? What differences between these two data sets lead to different ideas about average?

   b. What are Liza's, Thomas's, and Deon's ideas about the data that have the value of zero? (See lines 237–254.) Should these data be counted when figuring out an average? Why or why not?

3. In Suzanne's case 22, consider how Brynn counts and how Pat counts to find the middle on the second day (lines 387–395). What does each of these "middles" tell you about the data? Consider Josh's statement (line 396): "It doesn't matter, because they are the same. They're the same size, and they're in the middle either way." Do you agree?

4. Now turn to Alice's case 23.

   a. Consider the following students' statements about average: Amelia (line 613), Laura (line 616), Cal (line 636), Lex (line 677), Amelia (line 722), Richard (line 729). How are each of them thinking about the idea of average?

   b. Do you agree with Alice's conclusion (line 746) that "my class is perhaps finally in a position to start" interpreting data? Why or why not? Cite evidence from the case.

WORKING WITH DATA

Math Activity: Box plots

1. Compare the two box plots in each example (below and on the next page). What can you tell about the two groups? How do they differ?

2. Split your group into pairs. Each pair should make box plots for the Lost Teeth data—one box plot for the first grade, and one for the third grade. (Refer to the handout from Session 4 for the data.) When both pairs in your group are finished, compare your work. Discuss: How can you use the box plots to compare the two grades?

Box plots: Inauguration age data

Ages of 20th-century U.S. presidents and vice-presidents at inauguration

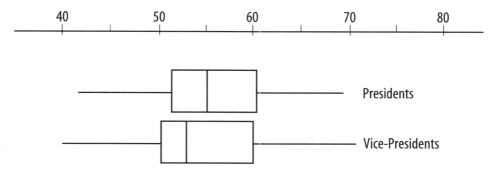

SOURCE: *Exploring Data,* Teacher's Edition, by J. M. Landwehr & A. E. Watkins (Parsippany, NJ: Dale Seymour, 1996), p. 72.

Box plots: Automobile air bag data

Make and model	Driver head injury	Driver air bag?	Make and model	Driver head injury	Driver air bag?	Make and model	Driver head injury	Driver air bag?
Acura Integra	585	No	Dodge Shadow	503	Yes	Mazda Protégé	779	No
Acura Legend	897	Yes	Eagle Vision	770	Yes	Mitsubishi Eclipse	772	No
BMW 325i	705	Yes	Ford Aerostar van	485	Yes	Mitsubishi Galant	1,024	No
Buick Century Custom	542	Yes	Ford Crown Victoria	907	Yes	Mitsubishi Mirage	919	No
Buick Regal	880	No	Ford Mustang	651	Yes	Nissan 240SX	407	No
Chevrolet Astro van	2,065	No	Ford Probe	784	Yes	Nissan Altima	610	Yes
Chevrolet Beretta	343	Yes	Ford Taurus	647	Yes	Nissan Maxima	818	Yes
Chevrolet Caprice	533	Yes	Ford Taurus wagon	480	Yes	Olds Eighty-Eight	473	Yes
Chevrolet Cavalier	770	No	Ford Thunderbird	541	No	Plymouth Acclaim	762	Yes
Chevrolet Corsica	493	Yes	Honda Accord	501	Yes	Plymouth Bonneville	359	Yes
Chevrolet Geo Metro	860	No	Honda Accord SE	555	Yes	Pontiac Trans Sport van	761	No
Chevrolet Geo Storm	417	Yes	Honda Civic	744	Yes	Saturn SL	705	Yes
Chrysler Concorde	770	Yes	Honda Prelude	510	Yes	Toyota Camry	390	Yes
Chrysler New Yorker	674	Yes	Hyundai Excel sedan	696	No	Toyota Celica	834	Yes
Dodge Caravan van	407	Yes	Hyundai Excel hatch	520	No	Toyota Corolla	522	Yes
Dodge/Plymouth Colt	919	No	Hyundai S coupe	870	No	Toyota Previa van	711	Yes
Dodge Daytona	399	Yes	Lincoln Continental	863	Yes	Volkswagen Passat	1,182	No
Dodge Dynasty	674	Yes	Mazda 626	589	Yes	Volvo 240	282	Yes
Dodge Intrepid	770	Yes	Mazda Miata	920	Yes			

These data reflect federal crash tests for 1993 cars sold in the United States. The cars were crashed into a wall at 35 miles per hour with a dummy wearing the seat belt and shoulder harness. A "Driver Head Injury" score of 500 or less means almost no chance of a driver getting a serious head injury. A higher score means more chance of a serious head injury. A score of 1,000 indicates about one chance in six. SOURCE: National Highway Traffic Safety Administration.

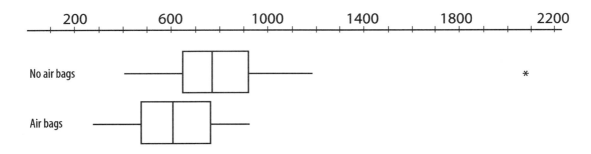

Driver head injury with and without air bags

SOURCE: *Exploring Data*, Teacher's Edition, by J. M. Landwehr & A. E. Watkins, (Parsippany, NJ: Dale Seymour, 1996), pp. 64–67.

Seventh Homework

Portfolio assignment: Reflecting on the cases

Look back through the casebook at the cases you have read so far for this seminar. Choose two cases that have helped you think about issues of learning and teaching in your own practice. Write about how these cases affected your thinking or raised questions for you about the important ideas in collecting, representing, and analyzing data. How do you think these ideas may affect your work with your own students? This writing can be primarily about the questions you are raising for yourself, rather than about any conclusions you have come to.

Reading assignment: Casebook chapter 8

Read chapter 8 in the casebook, "Highlights of Related Research." This chapter revisits the mathematical issues we have explored in the seminar, but this time from the point of view of educational researchers who have investigated the ways children make sense of ideas about data. The essay includes examples from the cases as well as examples from research. As you read the research essay, think about this question: How does this essay illuminate either the stories in the cases or the experiences you have had in your own classroom?

NOTE: You will be reading chapter 7 for the final session, *not* for Session 7. Reading chapters 7 and 8 out of order works better with the demands of the final data project.

Math assignments: Average price/Data project

1. Do the problems on "Averages, Part 1."

2. Continue working on your data project. In just two more sessions, your group must be ready to present your data project to the rest of the class.

Averages, Part 1

There are five bags of potato chips, each a different brand. All bags are the same size. The average price for all five bags is $1.38.

1. What could the prices of the five bags be? Think of at least two different sets of prices.

2. If both of your sets of prices included $1.38 as a price for at least one of the bags, now price the five bags *without* using $1.38 as one of the prices.

3. Did you use the median? the mean? If you used median, what is the mean for your sets of prices? If you used the mean, what is the median? Are they the same or different?

NOTE: We've worked on median in class, but we haven't yet worked on mean together. If you don't remember how to calculate or use the mean, don't worry. We'll work on this in the next class.

Displaying Data

Here are some guidelines for thinking about the representations you have been using in this course.

Line plot (or number line plot)

- Is straightforward to construct

- Makes the range, clusters, and gaps visible

- Lends itself to finding the median easily

- Preserves all the individual values in the data set

- Works best for a relatively small set of data (up to 30 or 40 values—some guidelines suggest only up to 25)

Stem-and-leaf plot

- Is straightforward to construct, once the conventions are understood

- Makes the range and clusters visible, but requires a decision about what intervals are best for the stem

- Lends itself to finding the median and quartiles easily

- Preserves all the individual values in the data set

- Can display a much larger data set than a line plot without becoming visually confusing; a guideline is up to about 250 values

- Allows back-to-back comparison of two groups

Box plot (or box-and-whiskers)

- Provides a *summary* of the data—does not show individual data values

- Highlights key features of the data—the median, extremes, quartiles—and allows these to be compared across groups

- Can be used with any size data set, including very large sets of data (although it is not useful for very small data sets)

- Is more complicated to construct; often a stem-and-leaf plot is constructed first in order to calculate the median and quartiles

7

The Mean / Research Highlights Essay

Session Agenda

Math activity ("Working with the Mean")	Groups of three	50 minutes
	Whole group	25 minutes
Break		**15 minutes**
Research essay discussion (jigsaw style)	Small theme groups	25 minutes
	Small mixed groups	45 minutes
	Whole group	10 minutes
Homework and exit cards	Whole group	10 minutes

Background Preparation

Read
- the casebook, chapter 8
- "Maxine's Journal," Session 7 (p. 197)
- the agenda for Session 7

Work through
- the math activity, "Averages, Parts 1 and 2" (p. 92 and p. 99)

Plan
- how to structure groups for the jigsaw research essay discussion

Materials

Prepare
- your responses to participants' sixth homework, "Students' Thinking about Comparing Groups"

Duplicate
- "Averages, Part 2" (p. 99)
- "Research Essay Discussion" (p. 100)
- "Eighth Homework" (p. 101)

Obtain
- connecting cubes
- large index cards or NCR paper (for exit cards)

Agenda

Math activity

Groups of three (50 minutes)

Whole group (25 minutes)

Through this activity, participants investigate how the mean is constructed and the relationship of the mean to the data set it represents. Participants also explore the different ways the median and mean represent the data—the median as a middle point in the data, and the mean as a point of "balance" or "evening out." Using two different representations of the mean gives participants a chance to view the relationship between the mean and the data set through different models. The cube model usually leads to a sense of the mean as an "evening out" of all the values in the data set; the line plot offers a model in which the mean can be seen as a point of balance in the data.

Small-group work Distribute "Averages, Part 2" and assign participants to small groups of three. Each group should have a supply of connecting cubes. Participants begin their small-group work by sharing their homework on "Averages, Part 1." As you listen to the discussions, make sure that groups move beyond talking about the mechanics of developing their lists of prices. You might ask, "How does the average, $1.38, represent the list of prices? How is it related to the five prices?"

Make sure that the groups consider at least one list that does not have $1.38 as one of the prices. Pay particular attention to how various participants created a list of prices in which the average was not also one of the prices. You may want to choose some of these lists for everyone to consider in the whole-group discussion. Note whether the groups used median, mean, both, or neither. What meanings are participants giving to the idea of "average"?

Prompt groups to move on to question 2 after about 20 minutes so that they will have about 30 minutes to work on the problems that focus on mean before the whole-group discussion. In question 2, participants develop two models of the data, a frequency distribution and a case value representation. They are asked to use these models to figure out the mean, rather than simply adding up the numbers and dividing.

Most adults know the formula for finding the mean, but have not thought through why and how this value can represent a set of data. Without insistence that they use the models, they are likely to add up the five values, subtract that total from 56, and distribute the difference between the two additional values. This method is perfectly valid, but if participants work only with the numbers, they may not stretch their understanding about the mean and its relationship to the data.

Questions 3 and 4 extend and generalize the work on the mean by varying the amount of peanuts in the additional bags and varying the target mean.

Everyone should work on questions 1 and 2 thoroughly. It is not critical that everyone move on to questions 3 and 4. If some participants work through question 2 quickly and seem to have a clear grasp of the mean and how it is modeled, you can encourage them to work on questions 3 and 4.

Whole-group discussion Focus the whole-group discussion on the models participants developed to show the mean. First consider the cube model. How did participants use cubes to figure out the problems? How does this model show how the mean is related to the data? How does this model help demonstrate what the mean represents?

Then consider the line-plot model. How did they use the line plot to figure out the problems? How does this model show how the mean is related to the data? How does this model help demonstrate what the mean represents?

By the end of this activity, some participants are usually feeling that the idea of mean in particular and average in general is pretty slippery. Why are averages useful? What does an average tell us about the whole data set? You might close the math activity with some discussion of these questions, including some discussion of the differences between the median and the mean. This is a good time to mention that the mean is more affected by unusual values in the data set. You could demonstrate how this works with one of the small peanut-bag data sets. For example, start with a set of 4, 5, 7, 8, 9, 11, and 12, and change the 12 to 26. The mean changes from 8 to 10, while the median remains stable.

Break
(15 minutes)

Research essay discussion (jigsaw style)
(80 minutes)

Small theme groups (25 minutes)

Small mixed groups (45 minutes)

Whole group (10 minutes)

Participants consider the research essay in a "jigsaw" format, which involves two steps and two different groupings. First, participants meet in small "theme" groups, with each group focusing on one or two sections in the essay. (See "Maxine's Journal," p. 202, for one idea about combining sections.) Next, participants recombine in somewhat larger groups, each with at least one representative from each theme group. (One technique for regrouping into mixed-discussion groups would be to have each small theme group count off, then all the 1's form a group, all the 2's form a group, and so forth.) In these mixed groups, participants will discuss the entire essay, section by section. You'll need to think through the organization of the small theme groups as well as the mixed discussion groups so that you have at least three people in each theme group and every theme is represented in the mixed groups.

Start by distributing the handout "Research Essay Discussion." After participants read through the description of the activity, answer any questions they may have and be clear about the time limit for the theme discussions.

Theme-group discussion Each theme group should discuss: What is this section (or sections) about? What examples from the research or the cases illustrate the theme of this section? Each small group member must be ready to discuss the section in the next small group. One pair of facilitators gave each theme group a recording sheet, with space to write a summary paragraph about that group's section(s) and to list specific examples of that theme from the cases. When participants moved to the mixed groups, they were well prepared to discuss their sections.

Mixed-group discussion Emphasize that this is to be a discussion, not a series of presentations. Those who have already explored a particular section in detail can initiate the discussion of that theme, perhaps give an example of the theme, and bring up any issues that were of interest in the theme-group discussion. However, *all* members of this group should be participating in the discussion of *all* sections. They have about 5–6 minutes to spend on each section. You might suggest that each group appoint a timekeeper.

Whole-group discussion Reconvene the whole group for the final 10 minutes and focus on questions like these:

- What was it like to read this essay?

- How did reading the essay differ from reading the cases?

- What was interesting to you about the essay?

- Were there ideas in the essay that relate to your own ideas about teaching and learning about data?

Homework and exit cards   (10 minutes)

Distribute the "Eighth Homework" handout. Spend a few minutes discussing how the project presentations will be structured during the next session. Answer any questions participants have about presenting and handing in their data project. You might mention that they will have one assignment— the final portfolio review—due after the last class.

Hand out index cards or NCR paper for the exit questions.

1. What is your understanding of the mean? How does it relate to the data? What does it tell you? What are your questions?

2. What did you get out of reading and discussing the research highlights essay?

Before the next session . . .

In preparation for the next session, read and write responses to the papers that teachers wrote reflecting on two of the cases they read during the course. For more information, see the section in "Maxine's Journal" on responding to the seventh homework (p. 206). Be sure to copy both the papers and your responses for your files before returning the work.

Averages, Part 2

1. Share one of your lists of five prices from "Averages, Part 1" with your group. How did you decide on your list of prices? How do you know $1.38 is the average in each example?

   NOTE TO EACH SMALL GROUP: Make sure you consider some lists that do not include a value of $1.38 as one of the prices.

2. Work through problems *a*, *b*, and *c* with your group.

   There are seven bags of peanuts. Five of the bags have the following numbers of peanuts in them: 5, 7, 8, 9, and 12.

   a. Make a representation of the five bags by using cubes. Make another representation of the five bags on a line plot.

   b. Now use your representations to figure out how many peanuts could be in the other two bags so that the mean number of peanuts in all seven bags is 8. Try to figure this out *without* adding up the peanuts in the five bags. Find at least two different sets of numbers for the two bags that will work to solve this problem.

   c. Revise your two representations—cubes and line plot—so that they show all 7 pieces of data. Can you "see" the average in your representations?

3. What is the least number of peanuts there could be in one of the additional bags? What is the greatest number?

4. What numbers could be in the two bags if the mean number of peanuts was 7? What if the mean number was 10?

Research Essay Discussion
A Jigsaw Experience

Step 1. Theme groups discuss one or two sections   (25 minutes)

Each small group has been assigned one or two of the sections of the research highlights essay as a focus for discussion. In your group, talk through the main points of the assigned section. Discuss specific points you found confusing or interesting when you read the essay. Refer to these by line number. Also locate examples from the cases that relate to the points made in the essay, or talk about examples from your own experience that are related to these research points. Take notes during this discussion so you will be able to share your group's ideas when you move to the second discussion group.

Step 2. Mixed groups discuss the entire essay   (45 minutes)

In these recombined groups, discuss the entire essay, one section at a time, starting with section 1. Allot approximately 5–6 minutes for each section. Since everyone has read the entire essay, this conversation should involve all members of the group sharing their ideas. Include examples and comments from your first set of small-group discussions at the appropriate times.

Step 3. Whole-group discussion   (10 minutes)

Talk together about the experience of reading and discussing this research essay.

Eighth Homework

Reading assignment: Casebook chapter 7

Read chapter 7 in the casebook for *Working with Data*, including both the introductory text and cases 25–28.

Portfolio assignment: Data project presentation

With your project group, get ready to set up your station to present your data project. Consider what you will need in order to make clear what you did and what you found out. You'll have time to circulate and look at other groups' presentations.

Then, you'll have a short time to summarize your findings to the group, to explain the issues you faced, and to hear questions and comments from others. It is likely that we will have this discussion in several smaller groups, so each member of your group should be prepared to represent your project.

You will also need to hand in a written report of your project (as a group), including any graphs or representations of your data.

Using Averages/Project Presentations

Session Agenda

Viewing the video	Whole group	15 minutes
Video and case discussion	Groups of three	30 minutes
	Whole group	15 minutes
Break and project setup		15 minutes
Project presentations	Looking at projects	15–25 minutes
	Project presentations	50–60 minutes
	Whole group	15 minutes
Reflection on the course	Whole group	15 minutes

Background Preparation

Read

■ the casebook, chapter 7
■ "Maxine's Journal," Session 8 (p. 210)
■ the agenda for Session 8

Preview

■ the video segment for Session 8

Plan

■ how to structure the project presentations. (Think about what room arrange-
ment will work so that you can first
have the video and case discussion and
then have participants set up their project presentations. An alternative is to
have participants set up their stations
as they arrive.)

Materials

Prepare

■ your responses to participants' seventh
homework, "Reflecting on the Cases"
■ a back-to-back stem-and-leaf plot of
the first- and fourth-grade height data
from the video, posted on easel paper
(see the Video Summary, p. 105)

Duplicate

■ "Video Notes" (p. 107)
■ "Focus Questions: Chapter 7" (p. 108)
■ "Final Portfolio Review" (p. 109);
before copying, fill in the due date and
your address, e-mail, or fax number

Obtain

■ VCR

Agenda

Through this session's discussion of the video and the cases in chapter 7, participants continue thinking about their own understanding of the mean in particular and summarizing data more generally. They will also be following student thinking about how to choose a single value to represent the "typical" value or average value in a data set.

Viewing the video (15 minutes)

Before showing the video, hold a brief discussion about the data you have posted from the video (first and fourth graders' heights). Given these data, how would participants answer the question, *How much taller is a fourth grader than a first grader?* Participants might talk in pairs for a few minutes, then share observations. Spend only about 5 minutes on this discussion. Keep the data chart visible, posted near the VCR, so participants can refer to it as they watch the video.

The video starts abruptly in the middle of a class, so you need to orient participants to the context for the class discussion they will see. Explain that this fourth-grade class has already collected and made graphs of the height data from the first and fourth grades. They also had a discussion that focused on describing the data. Now the teacher asks them two questions: *How tall is a typical first grader?* and *How much taller is a fourth grader than a first grader?*

Also before starting the video, distribute the "Video Notes" handout. Ask participants to take notes on each student's contribution. They will consider these students' ideas (along with the cases) in their small groups. Show the video segment without pausing for discussion breaks.

Video and case discussion (45 minutes)

Groups of three (30 minutes)

Whole group (15 minutes)

After the video, participants meet in small groups to discuss the focus questions for chapter 7 and the video. As you listen in on the small groups, decide what to use as the focus for a brief whole-group discussion. You may want to share ideas from the lists the groups make for question 1. Or, if participants are still thinking through what the mean is and what it represents, you may want to keep the focus of the discussion on questions 2 and 3.

Break

If groups did not set up their stations at the beginning of class, they should spend time during the break setting up their project for viewing.

Data project presentations

After break, allow 10–15 minutes for everyone to look at all the projects.

How you structure the discussion will depend on how many projects are being presented. In one seminar with four project groups, the facilitator allotted about 15 minutes for each group to present. For the remaining 15 minutes they discussed what had been learned from doing the projects.

In another seminar with more projects, the facilitator formed small groups with representatives from different projects. There were about four people in each small group, but not every small group had representatives from all projects. Projects done by pairs, for example, were represented in only two groups. This structure allowed each participant to talk about his or her own project for about 10 minutes and to hear about several others. The small groups met for about 50 minutes. Then the whole group reconvened for 25 minutes for general discussion, as above.

Whatever structure is used, project presentations follow this three-part format:

1. Give a *short* summary of the project and what you learned, keeping in mind that people have already viewed your presentation at your station. This is just to remind them what they saw there.

2. Discuss the issues you faced in your project work and what you learned about working with data.

3. Take questions from the group.

In the whole-group discussion, ask participants to reflect on what they learned from working on a project like this. How did the project work complement the learning that resulted from reading cases and doing math in class? Participants are likely to focus on their own learning as adults. At some point, you may want to ask the group whether anything they learned from doing the project has implications for their work with students.

Reflection on the course

At the end of this last session, provide a chance for participants to talk about what they have learned in the course, what goals they have for their students in working with data, and what questions they are still puzzling about. Hand out the Final Portfolio Review assignment, letting participants know when it is due and where to send it.

Once you have received all the Portfolio Reviews, write each brief note, commenting on their reviews, their data projects, and you want to mention about their class participation. It is not nece complete responses to the data projects, since you have been during the process and most participants will now feel finished with this effort. However, it is important to acknowledge the work they put into their projects by making a comment or two about what you particularly noticed in their work. For more information, see the section "Final Reflections" in "Maxine's Journal" (p. 215). Be sure to copy both the papers and your responses for your files before mailing them back.

S E S S I O N   8

Video Summary

Working with Data

Comparing Heights, 7 minutes

This fourth-grade class is looking at data they collected on the heights of fourth graders and first graders in their school. (Their representation is not seen on the video.) As the video opens, the class is in the middle of a discussion. The video shows student responses to two questions the teacher asks.

Grade 1		Grade 4
	4	
9 9 9 8 8 7 7 6	•	
4 4 3 3 3 3 3 3 2 2 2 1 1 0	5	0 0 2 4 4
	•	5 6 6 7 7 7 7 8 8 8 8 9
	6	0 0 2 4
	•	

The clip opens with four students responding to the teacher's question, *How tall is a typical first grader?* What follows is not a complete transcript, but captures the essence of what each student says.

JASON: I would say 53 or really close to it because that's the average.

TEACHER: What do you mean when you say that's the average in Rose's class?

JASON: That's what the most people . . .

TEACHER: The most common height?

GRADY: 51 or 52 . . . because if you looked at one of the graphs, there's an even number, so there's not one person in the middle, but if you used two, then one would be 51 inches and the other would be 52 inches.

The teacher asks how he would find that middle.

GRADY: If you put them all in a line and picked the one in the middle . . . shortest to tallest. You can't do that because there's an even number, so then you'd have to pick two people and one would be 51 inches and the other would be 52 inches.

SAMANTHA: I think that the mystery first grader would be just about 1 or 2 inches smaller than me . . . 51 or 52 or 53.

The teacher asks why she would think that.

SAMANTHA: Because some of the highest ones were taller than me . . . All of the first-grade heights came really close to mine, which is 53.

LLOYD: I think it would be 51 or 52 because if Rose's class has some of the highest first graders, then I think you should go into the middle heights of their class to find the height because that would be more of the average heights of a first grader.

The teacher now asks a new question: "Can you give me a number that says about how much taller a fourth grader is than a first grader?"

DEDE: I think 10 inches 'cause the tallest fourth grader is 64 inches and the tallest first grader is 54 inches.

TESS: I think that a first grader is 4 or 5 inches smaller. . . . I found the median of the fourth graders and first graders, then I just subtracted.

The teacher asks what the medians were, and Tess reports 57 for fourth grade and 51 for first graders. The teacher clarifies that the first-grade median was between 51 and 52 inches, so the difference is 5 or 6 inches.

Ralph also used an "average" for each group and subtracted. It is not clear what his definition of average is, but he may also be referring to the medians.

SAMANTHA: About 5 or 4 inches because the average first grader is 53 and the average fourth grader is 59 or 58.

The teacher clarifies that it is 58 or 57 (it is probably difficult to see the graph from where Samantha is sitting). Samantha says that she is referring to the most common heights.

LLOYD: I think we need data from all the fourth-grade classes and all the first-grade classes and then we need to see the most common fourth grade and the most common first grade.

Video Notes

This fourth-grade class is talking about their data on the heights of fourth graders and first graders in their school. As you watch the video, take notes about students' responses to two questions the teacher poses.

Question: How tall is a typical first grader?

Jason

Grady

Samantha

Lloyd

Question: How much taller is a fourth grader than a first grader?

Dede

Tess

Ralph

Samantha

Lloyd

Focus Questions: Chapter 7

Cases 25–28

1. In order to compare two sets of data quantitatively, it's necessary to find a way to summarize each data set. In the videotape you just saw and in Maura's case 27, students are comparing the heights of two groups. Make a list of at least five different measures or features of the data students use to compare. Cite an example from the video or from case 27 for each item and write a sentence for each to describe the mathematical ideas students are developing.

2. In Lydia's, Phoebe's, and Maura's cases, look for statements from children that suggest they have a beginning idea of the mean as an average. Find two or three examples of student ideas that you think are foundational to an understanding of the mean and explain why you think these ideas are important.

3. In Phoebe's and Nadia's cases, look for ideas that might get in the way as students begin to develop an understanding of the mean as average. Select at least two student ideas and explain why you see them as problematic.

Final Portfolio Review

Examine your portfolio from this course—your assignments and the facilitator's responses to you—and then write answers to the following.

1. Pick one area of mathematics you worked on in this seminar. Explain what you learned.

2. Pick one issue about student learning that you were thinking about during the seminar. Explain what you learned.

3. Quite likely, you are still puzzling about some issues, mathematical or pedagogical, that came up for you during the seminar. Pick one issue that is still "alive" for you; explain that issue and your current thinking about it.

4. Comment on what you learned from working on the data project.

5. What worked for you in this seminar? What changes would you suggest?

Due date:_____

Send to: _____

               _____

               _____

               _____

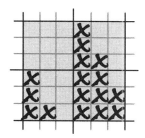

Data Terms: A Glossary

This section provides information about the statistical terms and data representations that come up in this seminar. The information is intended primarily as background for you, although you may find it useful to share parts of it with participants from time to time.

Types of data

Throughout this seminar, we refer to two types of data which we designate *numerical* and *categorical*.

Data that are *categorical* have values such as *yes* and *no*, *red* and *blue*, or *dog* and *cat*. These values cannot be compared or ordered as quantities. The order in which they are placed on a graph or table is arbitrary. While data such as these are sometimes designated by numbers—for example 0 for *men* and 1 for *women*—these numbers are only codes used to make recording easier. They cannot be added, subtracted, or averaged.

Data that are *numerical* have values that represent numerical quantities that can be ordered and compared mathematically. A respected statistics textbook by David Moore and George McCabe (1993) sums up the difference between what they term *quantitative* and *categorical* values, terms that correspond to our use of *numerical* and *categorical*. Their definition reads:

A quantitative variable takes numerical values for which arithmetic operations such as differences and averages make sense. A categorical variable simply records into which of several categories a person or thing falls. (p. 2)

Quantitative data is a useful alternative term for *numerical data*; you may want to introduce it to your participants.

Within quantitative data, further distinctions can be made. Not all numerical values behave the same way, and your participants may come across instances of data that they are not sure how to classify. For example, consider two data sets that appear to be numerical: family size and reading level. Values for family size can be ordered and compared in all the ways we might expect for numerical data: a family that has 6 members is twice as big as a family that has 3 members; a family with 4 members has one less person than a family with 5 members. We can find an average family size in such a set of data.

Reading levels may not behave in the same way. They can be ordered and have differences that can be calculated. A student with a reading level of 6.2 as measured by some reading scale is said to be reading 2.5 grade levels above a student with a reading level of 3.7. However, it may not be reasonable to say that a reading level of 6.2 is twice as high as a reading level of 3.1. It could be argued that we can't quantify "reading" in this way; it does not make sense to say "she is twice as good a reader as he is" if we mean that there is some quantity that is twice as great as another.

There are traditional classifications of numerical data that make finer distinctions among types of numerical data and provide rules about which statistical measures can be used in each case. You may have encountered some of these terms for data types—for example, *ordinal*, *interval*, or *ratio* data. However, this view of data types has changed in the past 30 years. Critics of the traditional classification of data types point out that while making these distinctions still has value, the classification has been applied too rigidly. What is most important is that we choose tools for analysis that make sense for the question being asked, not according to an *a priori* classification of the data.

As an example, let's do a thought experiment about grade level. Suppose there is a school in which there is one classroom of every grade from grade 1 through grade 6. Every Monday, a number from 1 to 6 is pulled out of a hat to see which grade will be in charge of making the morning announcements for that week. A graph is kept showing each grade level and how many times each has been chosen. In this case, grade level is a categorical value, a name for a particular group. We could just as well use the room number or the teacher's name.

At first, it doesn't seem that finding an average for these data would make any sense. But suppose some of the primary-grade students complain to their teachers that the fifth and sixth graders seem to get chosen a lot more than the other grades. We could simply count and compare the fre-

quencies for each grade, just as we would do with any categorical data. Or we might instead order the data by grade and find the median grade level. If it turned out to be grade 5, we would know that fifth and sixth graders were in fact being chosen at least half the time, while the other four grade levels were sharing the remaining weeks. Because our question has changed, we can treat the data values differently.

Yet another use of grade level might be in a study focused on high school dropouts in our town. We might collect information about the highest grade level achieved by town residents in their early twenties. Now we are using grade level values to indicate years of education and could reasonably calculate the mean grade achieved by people in the study.

In this seminar, when participants want to know if they have chosen data that are "numerical," they need to look not only at the type of data they are collecting, but also at their questions. Will their questions lead them to treat their data as quantities for which (as Moore and McCabe say) "arithmetic operations such as differences and averages make sense," or as categorical values that can only be counted and compared to see which data values occur with more or less frequency? As Velleman and Wilkinson's (1993) paper on this issue states, how we can operate on a data set "depends upon the questions we intend to ask of the data."

Value and frequency One of the issues that arises in the cases, especially in chapter 4, is that students need to sort out what the different numbers in their data mean. In Isabelle's case, "How Many People, How Many Teeth?" some of the second graders are figuring out how to represent the number of teeth lost by each person. Other students are trying to represent both the number of teeth lost (the values of the data) and *how many people* lost each number of teeth (the frequency of each value's occurrence in the data set).

Every data set has both values and frequencies. First, each piece of data has a value. This value might be a quantity such as 6 or a categorical value such as *yes*. In Isabelle's case, the values are quantities—for example, 0 or 1 or 5—representing the number of teeth lost. In Beverly's case, "Do You Like to Eat Soup?" the values of the responses are *yes* and *no*. In both cases, there are also frequencies—how many pieces of data have a particular value. There might be five students who have lost 3 teeth: the value of 3 occurs with a frequency of 5. There may be 10 students who responded *yes* to the question *Do you like to eat soup?*: the value of *yes* occurs with a frequency of 10. A graph that shows the frequencies of an ordered set of numerical values is called a *frequency distribution*. In Denise's case 14, Cara's graph is a frequency distribution, while Kenny's graph is not. (This is further discussed under "Types of Representations," p. 115.)

Terms used to describe and summarize data

Average   An average is a value that describes the center of a data set. In everyday usage, people usually assume that the word *average* refers to the arithmetic mean. However, *average* is also an inclusive term for any measure that is used to summarize the center of the data. Statistical references differ in the term they use to describe mode, median, and mean. They are all sometimes referred to as "averages," sometimes as

"measures of center," sometimes as "measures of location." *Mean, median,* and *mode* are further described in separate entries below.

Measures of variability   An average or center of a data set gives an incomplete picture of the data. We also need to know how the data are spread around the center, or how they vary. Two measures of variability are the standard deviation, used to show spread around the mean, and the interquartile range, used to show spread around the median. In this seminar, the interquartile range (the middle 50 percent of the data) is introduced informally when participants learn how to construct a box plot. Whether or not specific measures of variability are being used, it is critical that participants describe the shape of the data—how the data vary as well as where they are centered.

Mean   The arithmetic mean is a commonly used statistical average. It can be thought of as a "balance point" or as an evening out of the data. It takes into account all of the values in the data set.

One way to think of the mean is as the value that would result if all the values in the data set were evened out. This evening out is actually what you are doing when you use the algorithm for finding the mean. Finding the sum of all the values, then dividing by the number of values, results in the average. You might picture this as having a set of sticks of varying lengths. If we cut pieces off the taller ones and added them to the shorter ones until all the sticks were the same length, that length would be the mean value. It is as if we taped all the sticks together, end to end (added their values), then chopped this into the same number of even lengths as the original number of sticks (divided by the number of values).

Another way to think of the mean is like the fulcrum of a seesaw. If all the pieces of data were represented on a line plot, the mean is the point at which the number line would balance. In this model, the sum of the distances of all the pieces of data on one side of the mean from the mean value equals the sum of the distances of all the pieces of data on the other side of the mean from the mean value. Both the evening out model and the balancing model are explored by participants as they use cubes and a line plot with a small set of data (bags of peanuts) in Session 7.

Since the value of the mean is affected by the actual values of each piece of data, the mean is more sensitive than the median to unusually small or unusually large values in the data set. The mean is a less stable indicator of center than the median. However, in essentially symmetrical data sets, the median and mean will be close together.

Median The median is the value of the middle piece of data (or, in the case of an even number of data points, the midpoint between the two middle pieces of data). One way to think of the median is the value that would result if you listed all the pieces of data in order of their values and found the middle of the ordered list. The median cuts the data set in half. Half of the values in the data set are either equal to or greater than the median value, while half are either equal to or less than the median value.

The median takes into account all the pieces of data in the data set, but it is not subject to much change by unusually small or large values because the median depends only on the *order* of values, not on the actual values. The median is a stable indicator of the center of a data set and is often used for

data, such as housing prices, for which a middle value (rather than an "evening out") is most useful.

Mode The mode of a data set is the value at which more data occur than at any other value. A data set might have one or several modes. Modes are not generally used in statistics for the analysis of numerical data as they do not take into account all the values in the data and so may not communicate anything useful about the data set as a whole. In many data sets, the mode does not indicate anything of importance about the shape of the data. Mode is often used to describe categorical data, where the most frequent value may have more meaning ("the most popular TV program is . . . ").

Outlier An outlier is a piece of data that is well removed from the rest of the data. There are a variety of statistical procedures for determining whether a piece of data is small enough or large enough to be considered an outlier. In this seminar, we don't worry about the formal statistical definitions of outliers, but develop the notion that an outlier is a value to which we need to attend. It may be an error in the data or an unusual value of interest that should be investigated further.

Range The range of the data is the difference between the minimum and maximum values in the data set. These minimum and maximum values are called the *extreme values*. If the minimum value in a data set is 3 and the maximum value is 10, the range is 7. The word *range* is often used more informally to indicate the extent of values from minimum to maximum, so we say, for example, "the data range from 3 to 10."

Types of representations

The field of graphic representation is a lively and inventive one. For a glimpse into the many and varied ways of representing data, you might want to take a look at *The Visual Display of Quantitative Information* by Edward Tufte (1983). We encounter only a small sample of basic types of graphs in this course.

Of the common representations used by students in the elementary grades for numerical data, we see two major types, *frequency distributions* and what we have termed *case value plots*. Case value plots—such as Kenny's in Denise's case 14—show a bar or a line of counters for each piece of data. That is, each case (piece of data) is shown separately. The length of the line or bar indicates the value of that piece of data. A taller bar shows a higher value. A frequency distribution shows the number of cases at a particular value. The length of a line or bar indicates the frequency with which that value occurred. A taller bar shows more data.

On entering this course, participants may be most familiar with representations that are commonly used in the media, including bar graphs, histograms, and line graphs.

Bar graph   A *bar graph* is usually defined as a graph in which each bar shows a single value for one category (10 *yes*, 15 *no*; or 40 percent *yes*, 60 percent *no*). This type of graph is frequently used in the media to compare a few values.

Histogram   A *histogram* is often used to show numerical data in which there are many different values in the data set, making it impractical to show all the individual values. Each bar of the histogram shows a subset of the values. For example, the first bar might include values from 0 to 5 (equal to or greater than 0 and less than 5), the next bar from 5 to 10 (equal to or greater than 5 and less than 10), and so forth. The vertical scale indicates frequency.

Line graph   A *line graph* (as distinct from a *line plot*) represents a type of data that we do not treat in this course—data that reflect a relationship between two variables, showing how one variable changes as the other changes. One common example is a graph of temperature over time. Line graphs are used to show continuous change—change in which a variable moves through all possible values as it increases or decreases (e.g., as the temperature changes from 20 to 40 degrees, it moves through all the intermediate values).

In this course we emphasize several of the plots developed by statistician John W. Tukey and elaborated by Tukey and his colleagues from the early 1970s until the present. These plots—the line plot, the stem-and-leaf plot, and the box plot—are used for what Tukey termed *exploratory data analysis*—looking at a set of data to see its shape and patterns, to consider what it might reveal, and to generate questions for further study.

Line plot A *line plot* is a frequency distribution, showing the values of the data along the horizontal axis and the frequencies along the vertical axis. Each piece of data is represented by an X. The line plot is a straightforward way to represent every piece of data in the set in a way that reveals the shape of the data—where data are concentrated, how the data are spread out, where there are gaps in the data, as in this graph of family size in Maura's case 24, "How Many People in Our Families?"

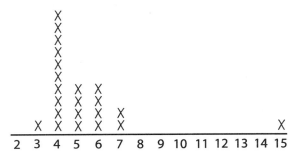

Stem-and-leaf plot A *stem-and-leaf plot*, sometimes called a *stem plot*, is constructed by ordering the data and arranging them in groups. Instead of X's or some other symbol, the actual values of the data are used.

A stem-and-leaf plot is particularly useful when the range of values is so large that it is not practical to use a scale that shows each value, as a line plot does. A stem plot is also useful when the data set is large; some guidelines suggest that up to about 250 values can be shown in a stem-and-leaf plot without becoming visually confusing.

In the classic stem-and-leaf display, the "stem" is the tens digit and the "leaves" are the ones digits, as in the plot of a group of teachers' commute times from home to school.

Teachers' commute times

```
0 | 5 5 9
1 | 1 5 6 6 7
2 | 0 0 0
3 | 4 5 5 5 5
4 | 5 5
5 | 0
6 |
7 | 5
```
3 | 5 is 35 minutes

For these commute data, grouping by tens works well to show the shape of the data, but for some data sets, the tens might be further subdivided, giving intervals of 5 or 2, as in the example of student heights.

Student heights

```
5 | 0 0 2 4 4
• | 5 6 6 7 7 7 7 8 8 8 8 9
6 | 0 0 2 4
```
5 | 2 is 52 inches

For data with much larger or much smaller values, the stem value might be hundredths, tenths, hundreds, thousands, or millions. In this case, the digit for the stem would be the next lowest place, and the other places would not be shown (the number is typically truncated). For example, following is a stem-and-leaf plot showing population of the 50 states, according to the 2000 U.S. census. The stem digit is millions and the leaves are hundred thousands. The rest of each number has been truncated. The key is used to indicate the values of the digits in the display.

Population of the 50 states (2000 census)

```
 0 | 4 6 6 6 7 7 9
 1 | 0 2 2 2 2 7 8 8 9
 2 | 2 6 6 8 9
 3 | 4 4 4
 4 | 0 0 3 4 4 9
 5 | 1 2 3 5 6 8
 6 | 0 3
 7 | 0
 8 | 0 1 4
 9 | 9
10 |
11 | 3
12 | 2 4
13 |
14 |
15 | 9
16 |
17 |
18 | 9
19 |
20 | 8
21 |
22 |
23 |
24 |
25 |
26 |
27 |
28 |
29 |
30 |
31 |
32 |
33 | 8
```

9 | 9 means 9,900,000
(numbers are truncated)

Back-to-back stem-and-leaf plots can be used to compare two sets of data, as for example to compare the heights of students in two classrooms.

Box plot A *box plot* (or *box-and-whiskers*) does not show each individual value in the data set. Rather, it provides a summary of the center and spread of the data. The basis of the box plot is the five number summary, which consists of these values: the minimum value (or lower extreme), the lower or first quartile, the median, the upper or third quartile, and the maximum value (or upper extreme). These values divide the data into four groups, with close to the same amount of data in each group. To find these five numbers, put the data in order, as shown in the example below. Find the median, which in this case is 13.5.

4 5 5 6 8 9 12 12 13 | 14 15 15 15 15 16 18 18 19

Then find the median of all the values below the median, which is 8—this is the value of the first quartile. Do the same for the values above the median to find the value of the third quartile, which is 15. The five number summary for this sample of data, then, is as follows:

lower extreme: 4
lower quartile: 8
median: 13.5
upper quartile: 15
upper extreme: 19

The left and right edges of the "box" are the lower and upper quartiles. The vertical line within the box is the median. From the box, the "whiskers" extend to the lower and upper extremes:

4 5 6 7 8 9 10 11 12 13 14 15 16 17 18 19 20

The *interquartile range*—a measure of spread around the median—is the distance between the lower and upper quartile values, which here is 7. So, the middle 50 percent of the data are spread within a range of 7 around the median 13.5. The interquartile range is also used to calculate outliers. One way to calculate outliers is as follows: multiply the interquartile range by 1.5. If a data value is more than this amount above the upper quartile or below the lower quartile, it is considered an outlier. Outliers in a box plot can be shown as separate points, rather than as part of the "whisker."

References

Moore, D. S., & McCabe, G. P. (1993). *Introduction to the practice of statistics.* Second edition. New York: W. H. Freeman.

Tufte, E. R. (1983). *The visual display of quantitative information.* Cheshire, CT: Graphics Press.

Velleman, P. F., & Wilkinson, L. (1993). Nominal, ordinal, interval and ratio typologies are misleading. *American Statistician 47,* 65–72.

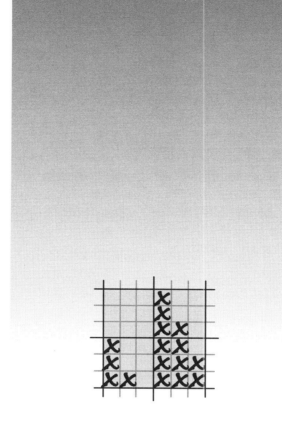

Maxine's Journal

Introductory note

"Maxine's Journal" was created to convey a sense of what a DMI seminar might look like—the type of discussions that can take place, the mathematical issues that may arise, the type of lessons seminar participants can draw from the sessions—and how it might feel to facilitate one.

Maxine is a composite character and so, too, are the teachers in her seminar. Though Maxine is fictional, her journal entries describe events and individuals observed and recorded by the developers of these materials and by those who piloted the first DMI seminars.

Because "Maxine's Journal" is based on early pilots of DMI, the specifics of a given session as Maxine describes it don't always coincide with the activities suggested in the agendas in this facilitator's guide. In particular, some of the focus questions and activity sheets were revised on the basis of feedback from the pilots. However, despite these adjustments, the major themes addressed in this seminar have remained consistent.

"Maxine's Journal" also includes examples of teachers' portfolio writing and Maxine's responses. Her responses may be longer and more elaborate than many facilitators would choose to write themselves. Even so, facilitators are advised to read these sections because they illustrate the kinds of issues that can be addressed through written communication between participants and facilitators.

October 4

Goals for the seminar

Next week I'll be starting the new data seminar. Twenty teachers are signed up from several nearby school districts, including an urban center, a small town, and a more affluent suburb. I know a few of them from other professional development projects, but most of them are new to me. They represent kindergarten through seventh grade, and the group includes two special education teachers.

There are several teachers of grades 5–7 in the group, and although there are no cases in the casebook beyond grade 5, there is currently so little done with data analysis in the middle grades, I think that the cases from grades 4–5 will be useful to these upper-grade teachers. I am also happy that we have such a strong presence of kindergarten and first-grade teachers (five of the twenty). I want the whole group to think about how students begin their work with data and how their ideas develop through the grades; I think these K–1 teachers will be able to contribute a lot. I know that primary-grade teachers can feel intimidated by what they perceive as the superior mathematical knowledge of upper-grade teachers; I will need to make sure that participants are able to listen to each other and learn from each other across the whole grade span.

I know that most elementary-grade teachers do some work with data, but in many classrooms this work is limited to making and reading a few different kinds of graphs—usually bar graphs, pie graphs, and line graphs. When data are collected by the students themselves, as is particularly common in the primary grades, graphs are often organized and posted by the teacher. The class may spend very little time describing and analyzing the data. I am expecting that ideas about data will be fairly unfamiliar to this group, and that they will need to spend time collecting, representing, and analyzing data for themselves.

In order to really experience how data can be used to answer a question, the participants will engage in their own data investigation during the seminar. I will give them some time in class to organize their groups and get advice from me and from each other, but most of their work will be done outside of class. The project will give them a chance to use some of the graphical representations and statistics they will learn about during the course. I am curious and excited to see how this aspect of the course will play out.

While engaging in data analysis as adults, participants will at the same time be learning about how children work with data. Through case discussion and through data work they do with their own students, they will focus on the important ideas children grapple with as they collect, represent, and analyze data. I expect that many of these ideas will be new to participants. I can think of five general areas that I hope participants will think hard about during the seminar: recognizing different types of data, designing data investigations, representing data, seeing a data set as a whole, and summarizing data.

Recognizing types of data

I suspect that participants have not thought about the difference between data that can be placed in categories and data that have numerical values. While we won't be getting into the distinctions between varieties of numerical data, I do want them to think about the basic differences between categorical and numerical data—what kinds of representations can be used to show each kind of data, and how each type of data can be summarized. [See "Data Terms: A Glossary" for more information.]

I've noticed in other professional development work I've done that some teachers believe at first that they can find a median in categorical data. They have not yet realized that the median can only be found in a set of data that can be ordered by value, and that categories do not usually have an inherent order (e.g., *dogs* doesn't come before or after *cats*). Participants will collect and describe categorical data themselves and will encounter cases about categorical data in Session 1 and Session 3.

In working with numerical data, students and teachers need to sort out what the different numbers mean and how they are related to each other. In the video for Session 1, participants will see second graders sorting out which numbers represent values (the number of pockets) and which numbers represent frequency (how many students have that number of pockets). In Session 4, participants will have a chance to explore these ideas in more depth.

Designing data investigations

I have recently done a lot of thinking about data analysis as the one area of mathematics that *always* takes place in a context. People collect data in order to answer a question or to illuminate some aspect of their lives. For this reason, every aspect of data collection and analysis must be evaluated in light of the purpose of the investigation. For example, was the investigation designed in such a way that it produced the needed data? Did respondents interpret the survey question in the way that was intended? Were the measurements accurate enough to be reliable? Does the way the data are represented in a graph or table give a view of the data that helps answer the original question?

I expect participants may be surprised at how much they need to think about in order to obtain the data they want. Session 2, "Designing a Data Investigation" will focus on this issue: how the design of a data investigation, including the questions that are posed, affect the nature and accuracy of the data that are obtained.

At the same time, I don't want participants to think that every bit of work with data in their classrooms has to be a major project that answers a question about a real problem in the school. Children are often quite engaged by straightforward questions about themselves and their environment and can learn a great deal about designing data investigations through work on such questions.

Representing data

In order to study the data we collect and in order to present those data to others, we need to make an organized representation. Every type of representation illuminates some aspects of the data better than others. We sometimes deliberately choose to obscure some aspects of the data in order to see others more clearly. Some types, such as line plots and stem-and-leaf plots, show every piece of data, while others, such as histograms or box plots, show summaries of the data. [These are further described in "Data Terms: A Glossary."]

In this seminar, I'll be introducing some representations that are likely to be unfamiliar so that participants can widen their own repertoire of representational tools while they also consider what problems in data display can be solved by different approaches. As they look at the representations made by children in the cases, they will see students inventing their own representations and also using standard types. I hope that, from analyzing these representations, they will see how children develop a sense that data can convey information and that organizing data in different ways can help clarify what the data have to tell us.

Seeing a data set as a whole

One key idea about data that develops across the elementary grades is that a set of data can be viewed and described as a unit. Young children start out by looking at each individual piece of data. In some of the kindergarten cases, children find it difficult to look at the data as a set of information about which they can make statements and draw conclusions. Gradually, through the primary grades, children begin to move away from their focus on individual pieces of data ("I picked pink" or "Ricardo picked green") to looking at larger parts of the data ("More kids had 5 pockets than any other number") and eventually to making summary statements about the whole data set ("75 percent of the fourth graders are in bed by 9:30"). For students and teachers, describing the "big picture" or the overall shape of the data is an important part of seeing the data set as a whole. I expect to emphasize this idea of the shape of the data in the mathematical work we do in class as well as in my responses to homework.

Comparing data sets—heights of students in different grades, amount of traffic at different times, number of students buying lunch when different menus are offered—shows the power of data analysis and often moves students toward seeing a data set as a whole. In Session 5, participants will focus on how, in the context of comparison, students describe and summarize data sets.

Summarizing data

I know that learning about averages is challenging for many teachers. It's likely that most participants will have learned how to calculate the mean but have not really thought about how the mean represents the data. The median may be even less familiar, even though they have probably encountered it in news reports. Since the way to calculate these averages is quite straightforward, it will be important to open up the complexity of what these statistics represent about the data and how students come to learn about them.

The use of averages and other summary statistics is a big leap in thinking about the data as a whole unit, not as a collection of individual values. How can you have an average value that isn't even one of the values in the data set? This is a quandary for both children and adults. By working on mathematical activities about average and reading the cases in chapters 6 and 7, participants will delve into these ideas.

The research highlights essay will offer another opportunity for participants to reflect on these ideas. Although there is not as much research about work with data, especially with elementary-grade students, as in some other areas of mathematics, the essay pulls together the research that exists as well as information that the cases add to this body of knowledge.

As I look forward to the first session, I have a lot of ideas—perhaps too many ideas—about what I would like participants to learn. I know I need to be flexible, to listen hard to the knowledge, concerns, and questions that participants bring to the seminar, and to slow down, ensuring that they have time and space to explore their confusions and build new ideas. I need to remember that participants will enter the seminar with a range of ideas and experiences, and that they will end the seminar with a range of new learning and growth.

I wonder what they are all thinking as they work on the preseminar mathematics assignment and read the cases in chapter 1.

Maxine's Journal

October 7

Last night was our first seminar session, and my head is already full, trying to remember all the new faces as well as all the issues that came up about understanding data analysis. Even though we mailed out directions and information about parking, quite a few people were late, so we got a late start. Participants are coming from schools with a range of ending times, so getting here at 4:00 is tighter for some than for others. Still, I will need to be clear that we start on time and that participants are expected to be here by then.

Introduction

I opened class with a few sentences about the focus of the course. Then I said, "A lot of people haven't had very good experiences with studying statistics in college, and some of you may feel uncomfortable remembering those experiences. Who has something to share about personal experiences with statistics or what it was like to work on the assignment that was due today?"

Barbara then said, "Well, I'm sure I did it wrong. I didn't know what kind of graph to make."

Sheila added, "Well, at least you thought of making a graph—it didn't even occur to me to put it in a graph. I guess I need this course!" Sheila laughed, and there was quite a bit of sympathetic and maybe nervous laughter from the group.

After a few more participants commented on the homework and about their previous experiences with statistics, Paul noted that he thought that statistics were untrustworthy: "Politicians use numbers to prove all sorts of things." There were a lot of nods in the group.

I worry a bit about the view that statistics can be used to say anything. I hope participants will come out of this course knowing that, while data can be distorted, they can also be useful. I decided to bring this introduction to a close by commenting on this point. I said something like, "So it seems important for you and your students to have a good grounding in these ideas so that you can use data well and can also interpret data that you encounter."

Math activity: "Well-known people" data investigation

Everyone seemed to enjoy answering the question, *With what well-known person would you like to have a conversation?* The activity served two important functions: It got the teachers immersed in collecting and representing data, and it gave people a chance to get acquainted. The question didn't require participants to reveal anything too sensitive, but it allowed everyone to express something personal and of interest to them.

We spent just a couple of minutes discussing what I meant by a "well-known person." I asked the group what that meant to them, and they raised questions such as whether the person had to be a real historical figure (for example, could it be a character in a book?) or whether the person had to be living. I confirmed that the person could be real or fictional, living or dead, and that "well-known" meant that it was reasonable to believe that the person had some public reputation and wasn't, for example, someone that only your family would recognize. I didn't want to have a long discussion about defining the question, since we will focus more on that idea in the next session, but I did want them to begin to experience how every question needs refining and clarification. I urged them to find a way to classify the information they would be collecting that would tell us something about our group. Even at this early stage, I want to keep in front of everyone that the purpose of collecting and analyzing data is to find out something about our world.

Groups got to work eagerly to develop categories for all the index cards. Having the names on separate cards allowed them to physically move the cards around as they thought about different categories. Several of the chosen "well-known people" were unfamiliar to some members of the group, so I urged them talk with the person who had made that choice, in order to learn something about that particular "celebrity."

Diana's group was thinking hard about what kinds of categories would tell us something about our group. They wondered if, because our group was mostly women (16 women, 4 men), more women would be chosen. They had sorted their cards into four categories: living women, dead women, living men, and dead men. To their surprise, more men had been chosen. Melissa commented that most of the living women were entertainers, whereas most of the dead women were known for their work on political or social issues. When I moved away from the group, they were engaged in a lively discussion about what their findings might indicate about today's society or about our group.

Some groups had one or two pieces of data that didn't fit in their categories. What do you do when this happens? Do you reconfigure your categories or leave out these data? Donald's group had four categories: social activists, political figures, entertainers, and pioneers. They couldn't decide where to put Toni Morrison. Nancy contended that she belonged with "entertainers" because people read books for relaxation and entertainment, but Rosa was adamant that she was a "social activist" because her books deal with issues of race, prejudice, and poverty. The discussion was taking on something of a "no, she isn't/yes, she is" quality without any reference to what we wanted to learn from the data. I asked whether they could decide on a phrase to define each of their categories and to reconsider what they wanted to ask of the data about our group. Rosa mentioned that it would help to know the intention of the person who had chosen Toni Morrison. Why did that person want to have a conversation with her, and what about her writing was significant? I thought this was an important issue to raise. After collecting some initial data, we can then become clearer about what we want to know and what our data will help us find out.

I had to work hard to move people into making their poster displays and getting them up on the wall in time for the whole-group discussion. Even though I had announced the time when they needed to have their representation posted, most groups hadn't even started their display when there were less than 10 minutes left. Most groups also had to be reminded to write some statements about their data, and they seemed to resist this writing. I wonder if their reluctance reflects a lack of confidence in working with data.

I gave the group a few minutes to walk around, looking at the displays. Then I brought everyone together and asked what issues had come up for them as they tried to organize and represent their data. Diana commented that after they had developed their categories of living and dead men and women, they began to wonder what their categories would look like if they asked everyone to choose someone currently living. Would they then still see the predominance of women entertainers, or would the group of women be more diverse? Several groups commented that further questions had come up as they looked at the data.

I asked Barbara to bring up an issue that their group had been discussing—one I thought was important for the whole group to consider. Barbara explained that they weren't sure what to do about the duplicate names. For example, three different participants had chosen Oprah Winfrey, so there were three cards with her name. Should they count her once or three times? I asked the group, "What would the difference be? If we counted each unique choice only once, what would that show? If we counted every card, what would that show?"

Larry immediately stated that "You have to count every card or you'll have wrong data—you might end up saying 'entertainers' are even with 'political figures,' but that wouldn't be right because you're leaving out some of the people who chose 'entertainers.'" His certainty seemed to stop the discussion; there were no other hands up.

Although in many ways I agreed with his view that if we are counting the frequency of each category, we need to count each response, I was concerned about the group dynamic of a confident upper-grade teacher providing "the answers," while more hesitant participants hang back. I decided to pursue this a little further. "So Larry's pointing out that if we want to be able to say something about how many of us choose people in each category, we need to count each card. The card isn't a duplicate because it's showing a different person's choice. But what if we did just use one instance of each well-known person chosen. Would that show something as well?"

Ellen offered, "Well, it would show something. It would show the kinds of people we picked, but not the numbers of people."

Annie added, "Yes, if we just wanted to find out who are all the people that we want to talk to, but not who are the most popular, we wouldn't count them twice."

Marilyn brought up another issue—that in organizing their data, they had to use a lot of their own knowledge. Helen added, "What we knew influenced how we saw the data. If we just knew one thing about someone, say that she was an author, we might just call her an author, but if we knew more about the person, we might end up putting her in another category."

I closed the discussion by commenting that work with data is in a context and that we need to know something about that context in order to organize and interpret that data. I mentioned a statistician I know who works in industry; he has to spend time in the industrial setting he is studying so that he will be able to design his study and interpret the results in light of the context from which he is collecting data.

Break and logistics

Just before the break, I gave out the handouts that explain the portfolio process, the homework for Session 2, and what to do about missing a class. I mentioned that there would be a reading and writing assignment for every class and that, in addition, participants would be working in a small group on a data project of their own choosing that they would present at the last session. I assured them that we would talk more at the next session about how to organize for this project, but that in the meantime, they should think about questions they might be interested in pursuing. I asked them to read the description of the project carefully, think about who they might work with, and come to the group with possible questions next time. I also mentioned that this was an opportunity for them to identify an issue or problem in their school that could be illuminated by collecting and analyzing data.

Case discussion: Students' ideas about data

After a brief break, I assigned participants to groups of three and four for the case discussion. Since I don't know many of the teachers yet, I had made up the groups in advance, making sure that each group had a range of grade levels represented. I also strategically placed a few people whom I knew from past work as reflective thinkers about teaching and learning.

I asked the groups to focus on questions 2 and 3 first. By focusing on Olivia's case, the group would get some experience with numerical data before they thought about their own projects. I told the group that I really wanted them to stick to the focus questions and try to answer them, but that they didn't need to rush through them. If they became embedded in one question and were thinking hard about some aspect of the children's thinking, that's fine. On the other hand, I really wanted to make sure that all the groups got to question 3, since question 3 focuses on the students' work whereas question 2 asks about participants' own math thinking. I decided that I would watch for this as I circulated among the groups.

I was able to listen to and participate in each group's conversation. I used this time to learn about the teachers in this seminar, both in terms of the ways they viewed children's thinking and in terms of their knowledge about data analysis. Most of the groups used the questions well and were able to establish a focused and participatory conversation. Occasionally, I would ask, "What line are you looking at?" to model using line numbers to identify specific passages, which helps everyone focus on the same thing. For example, at one point Suzanne was saying, "I thought they were really seeing the connection between the graph and the real thing when they were talking about how the pins would change all the time depending on what was for lunch."

I asked, "Can you find that in the case? What did they say exactly?" I want participants to get used to grounding their observations in specific evidence from the case.

One group was talking about Beverly's case, arguing about whether she should have given her students a yes-or-no question to answer. Carolyn was insisting that Beverly had limited the students' thinking by setting up the question in this way. I know that the opportunity to talk about the issues of setting up categories will arise again as Beverly's story continues with her cases in chapter 3, and I felt that this group had not yet focused on *student* thinking. Sometimes those who are new to reading cases tend to talk only about what the teacher did—and how to improve the teacher's approach. I want them to get used to using these cases primarily to think about how students interact with ideas about data. I asked them to move on to question 3 (they were satisfied with their work on question 2), and I remained with the group for a few minutes, helping them focus on the examples of student work in Olivia's case.

With about 10 minutes left, I found that another group was still working on question 2. They had gotten into a discussion about mean, median, and mode and how to find them using the set of data in Olivia's case. Larry had reminded the others of the algorithm for finding the mean, and they had done the math to get a mean of $7\frac{2}{3}$, but Helen and Lynda were looking puzzled. Helen said, "I don't see why $7\frac{2}{3}$ is the average. We must have done it wrong. Most of the data are below 7, and $7\frac{2}{3}$ isn't even one of the numbers."

I said, "You've noticed an important feature of these data—that most of the data fall below 7—and I see that you're trying to figure out how the mean relates to what you've noticed. We'll be doing a lot of work on different kinds of averages, including the mean and the median, in later sessions, so keep your questions in mind. In fact, you might want to write them down, so you can raise them again when we focus on these ideas."

Lynda asked, "But are we right that the mean is $7\frac{2}{3}$?" I said that it looked like they had done the calculation correctly, but that I really wanted them to move on to question 3 and focus on the students' thinking in the episode for the remaining time. Lynda didn't seem to want to let go of this conversation, but the group moved on.

Finally I called the whole group together and first asked them what they had noticed about the students' work in Olivia's case. Ellen began the conversation: "I was really surprised that the second group could talk about 'the most typical number.' That seems so sophisticated."

I wasn't entirely sure what Ellen was getting at, but I wanted to hear other comments. Barbara then said, "We were really wondering about how they made the scale on their graph. They included more numbers than they needed." It seemed that Barbara was going to stop there.

I said, "Can you or someone else in your group say more about what you thought about the students' ideas?"

Regina, who had been in Barbara's group, said: "It seemed like they weren't sure how high the data would go, so they were leaving room."

Donald added, "We thought that was a good idea, in case more data were collected later or you might compare the data to another group that had a different range."

I thought that I might want to remind the group of this conversation at some later time. It seemed to me to relate to the purpose of a representation: Is it a working representation to help you think about your data, or is it a graph to present final data to an audience?

Nancy then brought up a point her group had discussed. "We thought that the kids who made the first graph—Lauren, Tyrone, and Jacob—were really having problems. I think they have language processing problems."

I asked, "What were you noticing about their thinking?" Nancy said, "Well, the way they wrote 'most people in 9, 11, 12, 18, 7, 4 have a less.' They couldn't express their thoughts clearly."

Nancy is one of the special education teachers in the group, and I wondered if "language processing problems" was all she could see in these students' work. I asked the group, "What did you think Lauren and her group meant when they wrote 'most people in 9, 11, 12, 18, 7, 4 have a less'?"

Annie raised her hand and responded, "I just thought they meant that those values didn't have so much data. They noticed that a lot of the data were on 5 and 6, and all the other numbers had a lot less."

Rosa added, "At first I wasn't sure what they meant either. But when the teacher questioned them, Tyrone was really clear."

I asked, "Can you tell us what line number you're looking at?"

Rosa turned to the case. "Let's see . . . about line 265, actually it's Jacob first, and then Tyrone." She read out loud what Jacob and Tyrone had to say.

After a few more minutes, I moved on to looking at the data itself. I wanted the group to have an experience describing ordered, numerical data during this session. I put the line plot from Olivia's case on the board. I wanted to see how confident the group was about describing a simple numerical data set, and I wanted to give those who didn't know how to describe the data a chance to hear from others who did. I also knew this discussion would be an opportunity to introduce and define some statistical terms.

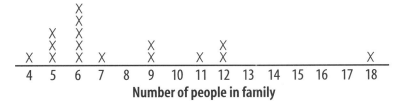

The group did a good job of pointing out the important features of the data, in particular, that a large portion of the data fell between 4 and 7. I wanted them to begin thinking about fractions or percentages of the data, so I asked about how much of the data that was. Several people answered that it was about $\frac{2}{3}$. Karen pointed out that you could also say that almost half the data were at 5 and 6.

There was also discussion about the outlier at 18, and we talked about what an outlier is. They came up with good ideas about why one might pay attention to an outlier: it might be incorrect; it might represent a misinterpretation of the question; or it might be a legitimate unusual value of interest. When someone pointed out that the "most" was at 6, I took a little time to clarify what was meant by *most*. Some participants clarified that it's not most of the data, but the value that occurs most frequently. I asked if anyone knew the statistical name for this, and the term *mode* was volunteered. Someone else talked about *range*, so that term was also introduced.

All in all, I felt this was a good start at describing numerical data. During this discussion, I did hear one comment to the effect, "It's the fifth-grade teachers who know all this stuff." The comment was an aside, and I decided not to put the person who had said it on the spot, but I realized that I was going to need to pay attention to the issue of lower-grade teachers feeling as if the upper-grade teachers are more expert.

Viewing the video: How many pockets?

I wanted to show the video, even though I knew we would not have time for discussion, and I let the group know that we would talk about it further in Session 4. I explained to the group my reasons for doing this—first, that I wanted them to have a visual image of a class doing data collection and analysis before they do their own assignment this week, and second, that I wanted to show them by example that classroom data work doesn't have to be an extended multiple-day project.

Participants were very attentive and seemed absorbed by the video. My bet is it will help them with thinking about the purpose of a data investigation. On their way out, I heard Rosa commenting to another participant about the teacher's wait time and how she stuck with one question and had students really think about it rather than just taking lots of different student responses.

If I'd had a few minutes to get reactions, I would have liked to hear some comments while they were fresh. I think I would have asked, "What did you notice? What struck you about the students' thinking? What struck you about the teacher's moves?"

Exit-card responses

For this first session, I asked people to write about their own experience as a participant in the seminar and about what issues in data analysis were on their minds. In looking over the cards, it's clear that participants were generally engaged, although at this point they had more to say about the seminar itself than about data analysis. Quite a few comments indicate how new data analysis is for them and that they are already thinking about how to approach this content in their own classrooms. Karen wrote:

> There is so much more to data than I thought. Collecting data and then interpreting it is challenging. I have questions of how to help students move to drawing conclusions from data.

Barbara wrote:

> I'm overwhelmed right now—I can't think of anything yet.

And Sheila told me:

> Never analyzed math before—the hows and whys. New territory
> which is a challenge! Even though I am phobic of math. I am
> wondering about what I can expect from my sped kids vs. regular kids.

Several comments about the video made clear that it indeed had an impact on some people's thinking. Donald's comment was typical:

> The video was fascinating to watch. Interesting how many children
> confused the data (pockets for people, people for pockets). Admired
> the children's focus and the teacher's prodding for clarity. Very
> interesting the shift from literal reading of data to deductive thinking,
> "jeans have 5 pockets."

Responding to the First Homework

October 10

It was fascinating to look at the teachers' work on representing and describing the set of data from two school districts, about years of teaching experience. Many of them used a double bar graph to show a comparison between the two districts. A couple of people used line graphs (an incorrect representation for these data), one used line plots, two said they didn't know how to represent the data, and two used some kind of list (which didn't show the data any differently than the original table they were working from). Even though most people had represented District A and District B separately, some did not separate them in their descriptions of the data. So, for example, Nancy wrote, "Nineteen years had the most teachers," including both groups in her statement.

Many of the teachers compared the groups in terms of *more* and *less*, rather than using fractions or percentages. In this case, the two groups do have similar numbers (41 and 43), so a statement such as "District A has more teachers with 16 to 25 years experience than District B" does capture something about the comparison. However, it is more accurate and more informative to say that about 55 percent of the District A teachers and 40 percent of the District B teachers have 16 or more years experience.

Overall, the responses showed little experience in comparing two groups and told me that quite a few of the teachers are not confident in representing data. In my responses to the assignments, I wanted to emphasize looking at the "big picture" of the data, to encourage use of fractions and percentages to describe clumps of data, and to comment on the representations used. In a few cases, teachers had used statistical measures, such as *mode* or *mean*, and I wanted to probe their understanding of these terms.

Judith made a double bar graph and wrote the following description:

- District A has more teachers with 16 to 25 years of experience than District B.

- District B has more teachers with 2 to 10 years experience.

- Both districts have teachers with from 2 to 25 years experience.

- They are nearly even in the 11–15 category.

- In District A there are no teachers at 1, 7, 8, 10, 11, 12, and 24.

- In District B there are no teachers at 1, 8, 15, 21, 22, 23, and 24.

- Neither district hired any teachers this year.

I responded to Judith:

Your first two statements capture a good sense of the "big picture" of these data. Looking at the overall shape of the data and summarizing where most of the data are is very important. Sometimes people lose sight of the big picture as they focus on particular measures, such as mode or median. You might want to think about using fractions or percentages to make your comparison even clearer. What percentage of teachers in each district have more than 16 years experience? I was curious about your statements about the values that have no data in each district. You've listed each value with no data. Are there particular groups of values in each district that stand out as having little or no data? For example, I notice that there are very few teachers with 7–12 years experience in District A, but almost 30 percent of the teachers in District B have this level of experience.

Judith also handed in a particularly thoughtful response to the first question on the preseminar assignment.

Judith
October 5

. . . I am coming to this course with the hope of improving my questioning skills. How can I help my students become better interpreters of mathematical data? Can my students get better at questioning themselves and others about what the data mean and improve their mathematical discussions and writing?

Answering question 2 was helpful because it required I spend a fair amount of time thinking. I realized that I could do the assignment in several different ways. I have questions about my teaching style: Do I allow students enough time to really ponder a question and to do the work necessary for making a visual representation? How do I evaluate the students' thinking and work? How can I be more aware of the characteristics of quality visual representations as well as the pace of my teaching? Finally, how can I get away from the thought that *time is a luxury in learning*? It is not.

While doing question 2, I engaged anyone who would allow me to do so. My downstairs neighbor had a peek at it, my husband was questioned, my baby-sitter was asked what she thought . . . Working with others often can take students to a new level of learning, which is where I want them to go.

I replied to Judith:

I find your musings very interesting, especially the idea that it takes time to dig into data, represent it, describe it, and interpret it. What can we get from quick (10–15 minute) data investigations in the classroom? How can such short investigations focus on an important aspect of data collection and description? For example, the video we saw in the first session is about 18 minutes worth of class work, yet a lot happens in that relatively short time. When do students need to spend several days or more on a data investigation? What ideas can they focus on in a more extended investigation? I'll be interested to see how your thoughts about this develop.

Helen had also used a double bar graph, but had barely any description of the data. Her only statements were:

- Everyone has been there for more than 1 year.

- 84 teachers total—43 in District A and 41 in District B

- More teachers are working during these years: 6, 13, 16, 18, and 19.

I responded:

Your first statement is a beginning step toward getting a "big picture" of the data. You could go further with this. For example, if you just look at District A, where are the data concentrated? Where is there not so much? I think you've made a start with this kind of description in your third statement, which lists the places on your graph where you see the most teachers. But instead of looking only at individual values like 6 or 13 or 18, see if you can look at groups of values. For example, for District A, there is a big clump of data between 15 and 20, or maybe between 15 and 22. More than half the teachers in that district fall in that range. If you looked at District A and District B separately, what would you say about the "big picture" for each district?

Diana had calculated the mean and the median for both groups. She gave their values, but didn't say anything about what those measures indicated about the data. As part of my response, I wrote:

You've calculated median and mean for both groups—what do the medians or means tell you about the data? How do the medians or means add to the other statements you've made about the data? (We'll talk about median and mean quite a bit later in the seminar, so keep these questions in mind.)

Maxine's Journal

October 14

From the first portfolio assignments, I saw quite a range of comfort with graphing and describing data. I decided to share with the group a few things that I noticed, both from their first exit cards and the first homework. First, I wanted to start them thinking about the importance of the diversity in our group and to point out that some participants who might think they had less to contribute (because they teach younger grades or special education) would in fact be important resources for the group. I read a few exit cards in which participants referred to their own grade level and what they hoped to learn about it.

I also read one or two cards in which participants wrote about already noticing that there was more depth to work with data than they had thought. I commented that having the span of grade levels that we did in our group, as well as some who teach special education students, would help all of us think about how these ideas develop in children across the grades. I said explicitly that even though some of the terms and formulas might be more familiar to the upper-grade teachers, we would all be trying to figure out the ways in which students come to understand the ideas represented by these terms and formulas.

Sharing homework

I circulated among small groups as participants shared the data activities they had done in their classrooms. Participants were interested in both what their students had and had not been able to see in the data. Quite a few talked about how students had begun refining or expanding their questions after they looked at their initial data. For example, Regina's fifth graders had collected data on the number of seeds in apples. After they looked at their data, they began wondering whether the size or kind of apples would affect their data. The students concluded that they would have to collect much more data in order to draw conclusions about the number of seeds in apples.

Another group had an interesting discussion about how to know if data are accurate and reliable. Karen had asked her second-grade students what vegetable they found most detestable. As students were giving their responses, one student wanted to know what Karen's most detestable vegetable was. When Karen explained that she doesn't have one any more, but that when she was their age, it was onions, a lot of students wanted to change their answer to onions. The group talked about whether the children had changed their answers because they wanted to be like the teacher. Annie talked about the distinction between gathering data on buttons—something she saw as pretty objective—as opposed to gathering data about opinions, or something as subjective as what types of vegetables you hate. She suggested that you could list one vegetable but then after hearing another person's vegetable, think, "Yeah, I really do hate that one." It seemed to me that the group was focusing on an important issue about measurement in data: How do you make sure respondents have considered a range of possible responses without limiting or influencing their answers?

Although it seemed that participants could talk longer in these groups, I wanted to make sure that we had enough time for both the case discussion and the math activity, so I gave the groups a 5-minute warning and ended after 25 minutes. They had had the chance to share work from their own classrooms and to see how issues raised by the cases and in the mathematics we do together come up with their own students. I also hoped that spending this time on the homework would reinforce that the work they do outside of class is important in developing the ideas of the seminar.

As a transition to the case discussion, I asked to just hear a sentence or two about issues that had come up in the small groups. Several had discussed the idea that questions needed clarification before data were collected and that initial data often led to a new or redefined question. Diana said that her group had talked about how we know data are accurate and reliable. "In fact," she said, "are data *ever* accurate and reliable?"

I was especially interested in the murmurs of assent and nodding heads that I noticed as Diana mentioned the last point. I think the group is beginning to confront the issue of whether or not data are "facts." I knew this would come up, and I always worry about how easy it is to take the view that all data are unreliable and therefore can't tell you anything. Sometimes I hear this as the view that "anyone can lie with statistics," therefore all statistics are lies. I will have to help participants realize that, on the one hand, data can never give the complete, "true" picture, but that, on the other hand, we can use sound data collection and analysis methods to learn something. I think it is difficult for many of us to get used to the idea that we are dealing with uncertainty, and that we are trying to capture something that can never be completely captured.

Case discussion: How purpose helps define questions

I decided to keep the same small groups for the case discussion to minimize the time for reorganizing. I planned to spend about 20–25 minutes in small groups, depending on how the discussions went and how much time I felt we needed to spend in the whole group. I hoped that participants would see connections between the cases and the work they had done with their own students.

For focus question 2 (about Sally's case 4), I observed some very different kinds of discussions. Some participants were quite uncomfortable with the emotional/social issues raised in Sally's case. In one group, Lynda was arguing that the teacher should have anticipated the potential problem and should have protected Jean Pierre and Eddie from feeling that they didn't belong to the group. Barbara felt that the teacher handled the situation well, but expressed concern about students who might not understand how to answer a data question. This group as a whole seemed to be concluding that students should be sheltered from experiences in which they are, as Lynda said, "put on the spot."

However, Annie's group had a very different view of the episode. They thought that the students must have had a lot of practice in carefully defining data questions because they were so clear about what "counted" as having milk for breakfast—for example, that milk in coffee counted. They thought that the teacher had handled the issue well, making it clear that someone could change their answer and that the goal was to collect accurate data, not to have a particular answer.

As some groups moved on to focus question 3, I noticed a similar range in the various discussions. Some participants thought that Natasha has a complex idea about defining the question that she can't quite articulate. Others thought that Keith's approach is "right" and Natasha is "confused."

I decided to spend some time on these issues with the whole group so that participants could hear the range of opinions. I felt that some participants in groups with someone who held a strong opinion might not be getting the chance to work out their own thinking. But I also wanted to make sure that we got back to the main idea of the cases: the connection between the question that is asked, the data that are collected, and the purpose of the investigation.

When we gathered as a whole group, I said that many small groups had talked about the students who changed their answers in Sally's case and that I wanted to hear more about the issues that had been discussed. Lots of hands were up, and I called on Barbara. I knew she had expressed concern for the two students, but didn't seem to have a rigid view about what the teacher should have done. She pointed out that if students don't know how to answer a data question they will feel left out of the group and won't be able to engage in the work about the data. Sheila then said that she thought that the teacher needed to make sure questions were chosen carefully and worded clearly so that students wouldn't find themselves in an uncertain position.

I then asked, "So what do the rest of you think about the choice of question and how it was worded?"

Annie said it seemed to her that it was important for the students to work on defining the question rather than always being given a question already formulated. Ellen agreed and added that the students in Sally's case seemed to understand that they had to work at defining their data question. Sheila seemed perplexed and unsatisfied as she said, "Well, then, I think you have to choose questions that won't get you into these issues where a child might feel left out."

I said, "I can imagine that, as a teacher, I would have thought that this question was pretty benign."

Regina volunteered that she had done her assignment using the question *How many pets do you have?* and that some of the students in her class didn't have any pets. She helped them understand that the number of people with no pets was an important part of the data, that they would be doing a lot of surveys, and that for different questions, different people would probably have answers of "zero." Regina concluded by saying that she didn't know how all the children ended up feeling, but that she thinks that if they make data collection a regular part of the class activity, students will get more used to being part of the data on a variety of questions. She also thought that a couple of students were inflating the number of pets they had so that they would have the most—so that they would "win." Donald observed that it would probably take a while for students to learn about the importance of accurate data.

At this point, I felt that enough ideas about the emotional issues connected to data collection had been aired and I turned the conversation to Natasha and Keith in Andrea's episode. I asked everyone to look at lines 339–348 where Natasha is explaining her idea. Several participants thought that Natasha was working hard to define what it meant to "visit" a state, and that she clearly wasn't satisfied with simply passing through a state—she was after something more substantial. Marilyn added that it would be important to support this kind of thinking rather than letting students with a more complex idea, like Natasha's, be overrun by others. Nancy, one of the special education teachers, mentioned that she often sees students like Natasha who have good ideas but don't articulate them very well, and that these students are easily pushed aside by other students who are more forceful. Carlos summed up the conversation nicely by saying that Natasha had a *purpose* in mind, and that maybe Keith just wanted to fulfill the assignment.

I feel it's important for ideas about the emotional issues embedded in data collection to surface early in the seminar. Because data are always from some real-world context, students often have some stake in the data they are collecting. It may be that they don't want to look different from others; it may be that they want to be the best or have the most; it may be that they are reluctant to share the truth about some aspect of their lives; or it may be that they have a certain point of view about an issue that they are determined to defend. Teachers need to be aware of all these possibilities, yet also realize that it is impossible to work with real data about the students without bumping up against some potentially sensitive issues.

Math activity: Surveys of our group

I had several agendas for the math activity: I wanted to give participants more experience in defining a question and connecting the data to the question; I wanted to give them more experience in using line plots and describing numerical data; and I wanted to discuss the difference between categorical and numerical data. I kept in mind that I needed to reserve a full half-hour to organize participants for the data project, so I was careful to keep the opening group activity to 25 minutes.

I pointed to the question I had written on the board: *How many years have you been teaching K–12 students?* I asked the group to think about the question for a minute, to think about how they would count the years for themselves, and to come up with any ways in which they think the question should be refined or clarified. The group came up with lots of questions, which I quickly listed in abbreviated form on the board. Their questions included:

Does subbing count?

Is summer school a year?

Do we count student teaching or internships?

Should we count this year?

What about teaching a sport?

After we'd listed quite a few questions, I asked, "What would be your decision on one of these questions, given what you'd like to know about our group in terms of our teaching experience?" In retrospect, I think I should have had participants talk about this question in pairs for a minute or two, giving more of them a chance to verbalize their ideas. But there were some good comments here: Carolyn said that subbing should count, because many people spend significant amounts of time as long-term subs and that is part of their teaching career. Diana said that she wouldn't count internships or student teaching; she's more interested in how long people have been teaching as a career—that is, not when they're in training, but when they're actually working.

I know that this kind of conversation can go on for a long time and that it's difficult for a group of twenty to come to consensus. After a few more comments, I said this directly to the group. I went on to say that I was going to define a question for the group myself so that we could proceed to collecting and describing the data. As always, this initial data would probably give us ideas about what might be most interesting to pursue and how to refine our question. Building on what some of the participants had said, I said we'd count the number of school years spent actually being paid for working as an educator in a K–12 school. Participants could count parts of years or prorate part-time work. I saw a few people ready to ask more clarifying questions, so I said that they could make their own decisions about how to count on any other points of which they were unsure. I collected our data on a line plot on the board.

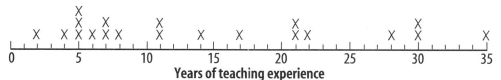

Years of teaching experience

I formally introduced *line plot* as the term for this representation. Since time was running short, I decided not to have much discussion on what the data actually showed. The focus of this session is on defining questions, and I thought that our discussion had helped people focus on this issue. I simply asked everyone to spend a minute writing down one or two statements that would help describe the "big picture" of these data. As people finished, I asked them to compare their statements with someone near them. After about a minute, I asked for a few volunteers to offer their statements. We ended up with these statements recorded on the board next to the graph:

> The range is from 2 to 35 years.
> More people are on 5 than on any other number. The mode is 5.
> About half the group has between 2 and 11 years of teaching experience; the other half has between 14 and 35 years.
> There's a bunch of data close together at the beginning, then the rest are very spread out.

I thought about commenting on the fact that even though the mode is 5, it doesn't show anything particularly significant in this set of data, but I decided that we'd done enough with this data set for now, and I wanted to move on to the rest of the activity. I'll need to remember that this point should come up at some other time. I worry that people learn a term like *mode* and simply use it without thinking about whether it indicates anything important about the data.

Small-group survey To prepare for today's survey work, I asked participants to volunteer some of the questions that they had thought of for homework. I had two goals for this brainstorming: (1) to give them ideas for both today's survey and for their project; (2) to help clarify the difference between numerical and categorical data. I know from experience that it's often difficult for teachers to make this distinction. It all seems numerical to them, because *numbers* are involved in any kind of data collection. That is, if we ask *Do you like chocolate?* there will be some number of *yes* responses and some number of *no* responses; numbers are used to count the frequency of each response. But the *values* of the data are categories—in this case, *yes* and *no*—not numerical values. If the question is *How many sisters do you have?*, the response is a numerical value—the values of the data are expressed as quantities that can be ordered.

I asked the group to look carefully at the questions and think about what kind of answer they would give to each—would it be a numerical value like 3 or 12, or a categorical value like *yes, no, chocolate, vanilla?* Then we quickly went down the list, jotting sample responses to each question.

How much sleep do you get? How much sleep do you need? *8 hours*

How many pairs of sneakers do you own? *3*

What pets do you own? *dogs and cats; 2 cats and 1 dog*

How much time do you spend reading per day? *1 hour*

How many e-mails do you get per day? *15*

How many hours of exercise per week? *2.5*

What states have you lived in? *Massachusetts, Illinois*

I then asked which questions had categorical answers. They easily recognized that the last question did not result in numerical responses, but would if the question were changed to *How many states have you lived in?* There was a little discussion about the pets question. Participants pointed out that if you asked the question the way we had written it on the chart, you might or might not get a numerical response. If you asked *How many pets do you own?* or *How many dogs do you own?* you would get a numerical value.

I reminded them that today—and for their projects—they'd be choosing questions with numerical responses because I wanted them to have experience with the kind of representations and data tools, such as averages, that can be used with numerical data.

To form groups, I asked if anyone already knew which question they wanted to use for today's survey, then asked if others wanted to join them. This resulted in three groups of four. The rest of the participants I then arbitrarily put into two more groups of four.

The surveys went smoothly and all the groups got their representations posted. To wrap up, I gathered everyone and asked each group to address two questions: Did the data you collected give you information about your question? Given your initial results, would you now want to revise your question, or do you have a new question that you would like to pursue?

One group had already modified their question. They started out by asking how many TVs each person owned, but soon heard many people respond that they wished they had either more or fewer than they actually did. So they asked everyone a revised question: *How many TVs do you wish you owned?*

Since the word *average* had come up in a number of groups, I decided to at least open up this idea. I remarked, "I heard some of you saying that there's something strange about an average of 2.5 pets, when you can't have half a pet. So who has an idea about what this average, 2.5, tells us about this set of data?" There was quite a long pause, and I got the sense that most people weren't ready to tackle this question.

Marilyn then raised her hand and said, "I think it just gives an idea of about how many pets most people have."

Rosa contributed, "It's not exactly 'most,' because nobody has 2.5 pets, but most of the people are around that number—like a lot of people have 2 or 3."

Ellen then raised her hand very tentatively and said, "If I see something in the news, like Americans eat an average of 50 hamburgers a year, then I don't think that everybody eats 50 hamburgers—vegetarians wouldn't eat any, and some people might eat a lot more. The 50 is sort of where it all balances out."

This was a great comment to end with, and although there were now several more hands up, I said that I'd heard several ideas about average: a value or a range of values that occurs the most often in the data set; a way to balance out all the different values. I asked the group to keep these ideas in mind, to keep thinking about the idea of average, and said that we'd be doing quite a bit of work on these ideas starting in later sessions.

Organizing for the data project

Next we turned our attention to the data project for this seminar. Three groups, each composed of teachers from the same school, had already decided to work together. Everyone else finally organized themselves into several small groups or pairs. I gave them until 5 minutes before the end of the session to talk about their question, to make sure they had exchanged contact information, and to begin making plans for their pilot investigation.

As I interacted with each group, I could tell that some participants were feeling overwhelmed by the idea of a "pilot investigation." I told them to keep it small—to think of this as testing out their question. Some people wanted to know how much data they needed to collect for their pilot and whether they could use the same people again in their final study. I suggested that they include at least 20 or 25 pieces of data, and that they probably couldn't answer the second question yet. I reminded them that their question might change quite a bit after their pilot investigation.

Exit-card responses

In looking over the exit cards, I was glad to see that most participants were focusing on issues of how to support students' work with data and were connecting what they were reading in the casebook to their own classroom work. For example, Barbara wrote about her reaction to Andrea's case 6 ["What Is in a Question?"]:

What stood out for me was having students create their own questions. I didn't think my students would be capable of this, but found, through our discussion on favorite spuds, that I was wrong. I underestimated them again!

Sheila was one of the few who had very little to say. She wrote:

The cases were good, mostly for discussion.

I wonder what her cryptic response signifies; she isn't very vocal in class, either.

Suzanne focused on the emotional issues raised in Sally's case 4. She wrote:

I felt badly for Jean Pierre who sheltered under the table, unfortunately feeling self-conscious about breakfast and his chosen response. I have children who participate in the breakfast program at my school and others who are eligible to participate but whose parents refuse. Even kindergartners are aware that breakfast is usually eaten at home and are somewhat self-conscious about having to eat breakfast at school. Breakfast can be a sensitive issue for many kids and families.

I don't know Suzanne well enough yet to know whether she is using this focus as a way to avoid digging into students' thinking, or whether this breakfast issue is one, as she explains, that is particularly salient for her students. As part of my response to her homework, I need to acknowledge that it's important to be sensitive to students, but that you also can't eliminate all data questions that involve personal responses. I'd want to pose the question, "How can data collection and description become a routine part of classroom mathematics in which students can participate easily?"

Responding to the Second Homework

October 17

As I read participants' portfolio writing about doing a data activity with their students, it was clear to me that many of these teachers had previously done very little work with data in their classrooms. A surprising number expressed dismay or frustration at how little students were able to see in data they had collected. One goal of my responses would be to point out beginnings of student thinking about data and to remind them that their students need to collect, represent, and analyze data regularly in order to gain experience. Melissa's writing raised a number of issues.

Melissa
October 12

My first impression of this assignment was, "Oh, this looks easy. Pretty straightforward." I couldn't have been any more wrong. In my rush to get this activity in with the limited amount of time I had, I chose the subject of the data activity and presented the question to analyze it. The children were asked to look at the data and to answer this question in writing: "You are the Program Director at your station. What would you do with this information? What is it telling you?"

My Favorite Television Show

I was surprised that many students used the information to determine what day and what time each of the programs should be aired, but they gave no explanation for their choices. I needed to know why. Unsatisfied with the results, I returned the papers to them and asked them to re-examine their work and to justify their programming choices. I got lots of explanations, but few that were based on the data. Most gave their personal choices.

"I will pick Rugrats in the morning and evening because lots of kids like the show and even babies because the show is about babies and kids."

"In the morning I would show cartoons like Arthur, Rugrats, Pokemon and Digimon. I put it in that order because they are animated and they are funny."

Many of the responses used this kind of reasoning. Only one or two students actually focused on the data.

"I think I would put the bad ones, the ones with the littlest Xs last because children will not watch it as much."

I know we need to do a lot more talking about this activity, but also I need to allow the students to pick the focus and generate the question.

When I read Melissa's paper, I was concerned that she was trying to connect data that were collected for one purpose (to indicate the students' favorite TV show) to a different purpose for which the data were not well suited. I needed to strike a balance between providing some encouragement and helping her consider the connection between data and purpose. Her episode also brought up an issue that concerns me. Often I see upper-grade students doing the same simple collection of categorical data that they did in first grade. I knew that working with data was new for Melissa, but I wanted her to think about using numerical data with her fifth-grade students.

Dear Melissa,

I don't think it's surprising that students aren't very skilled at making arguments based on data. This is a complex skill, and it will be interesting to follow what happens with your students as they have more experiences with data. This also might have been a pretty complicated question to use at the beginning. I'm not sure I'd be able to figure out what these data could tell a Program Director. I think the students are thinking about some pretty sensible arguments, based on their experience, rather than on the data—for example, young children watch TV in the morning, so that's a good time to schedule cartoons.

An important feature of your data is that it is pretty "flat"— there aren't big differences in the number of people who picked the various shows.

I think it will be interesting to see what happens with another question. You might want to try a question that involves numerical data—*How many people in your family? How long does it take you to get to school?*

Maxine

At the other end of the grade range, Ellen wrote about her pre-kindergarten class. I thought she was asking an important question about how much to guide her students' first forays into working with data.

Ellen
October 11

The issue that came up for our class in our investigation of *Today's Question* was the issue of organization. Each child individually answered the question *Do you like bananas?* by putting a purple cube in the Yes box if they did, and a yellow cube in the No box if they didn't.

We then dumped the contents of each box into a pile to examine. I posed the question: "What do you notice?" Several children wanted to tell me that "The kids who liked bananas put in a purple cube and the kids who didn't put in a yellow cube." Others were very intent on explaining why you might like bananas, but you didn't have to. I could have laughed at myself out loud. I have a mix of 4- and 5-year-olds in my class—some very young—and their very nature is to state exactly what they have done. It's a 4-year-old thing. I should know better than to pose a question like that to the kids in the beginning of the year.

My next question was, "How can we find out how many people chose YES and how many people chose NO?" Several students thought we should count, so for each answer one student counted the pile, then we double-checked by having a second student put the cubes into a stick and count again. Less important was the fact that 13 children chose YES and 6 children chose NO, but right after both sticks were assembled, several children burst out with "Lots of kids chose YES," or "More people like bananas."

That got me thinking. Would there have been more of the "response that I was looking for" if I had posed the "What do you notice?" question when the cubes were in sticks? I thought that it might. So, should I guide the data we gather into sticks and other more organized collections before we discuss them, or is it more important for children to see the process of organizing the data into a way that is easier to work with? I guess my inclination is the latter, but I would love to talk it through with someone (or several people).

Dear Ellen,

I still like the way you posed the question at first: "What do you notice?" Even if this didn't lead to suggestions to organize the data, it gives you information about what students do think about what they are doing. This is always useful, and it will be interesting to see how responses to this question might change as the children's experience with data increases.

I think your second question was also good—at that point, it pushed students to think about organizing the data. I don't think there are any rules here about which approach (organizing the data first or having the students organize the data) is better. Students are going to need to see a variety of models of organizing data so that they begin to build up ideas about how to represent data and about how to "read" those representations. At this point, they could probably benefit from sometimes filling in charts or using clothespins on a Yes/No board, for example. But at times I think it would be good to experiment to see what their ideas are about organizing the data.

I'll be interested in hearing how their ideas progress as your students have more experiences with data.

Maxine

Maxine's Journal

October 21

To begin class, I reviewed a few overall things that I'd noticed about the homework. Even though I'd given everyone individual feedback, I thought it would be useful for them to hear that some themes were appearing across their work. Then I asked the group to briefly share the questions they were pursuing for their pilot study.

Group norms discussion

We'd been meeting together long enough that it was time to consider how we were functioning as a group. As in most groups, some participants were very active, while others were relatively silent. Some people had a tendency to overpower others in small groups, while a couple seemed closed to ideas different from their own. Airing what helps everyone participate in the group often helps these teachers become more aware of their own and others' needs. It also lets me know if there are issues I need to think about in order to help the group become a learning community. Even if some people didn't speak up in the group discussion, I hoped that *having* the discussion would make it possible for those with concerns to write to me on the exit cards.

Rosa started the discussion by commenting on her own experience: "There's a certain perspective you get by being a student." I asked her if she could say more about that or if anyone else wanted to elaborate. Regina said that she was beginning to feel that she could show her own ignorance, because there were enough other people who admitted that they didn't understand things, too. Everyone laughed at this, and then Regina added, "At first I was very careful about showing that I was confused half the time, but in the small groups, it was easier to get involved."

Paul volunteered, "Whatever we are saying in the small groups, people are valuing."

I asked, "What is it that helps you feel safe to dig into ideas in the small groups? Are there things that we can be conscious of to make this happen?"

Larry, the seventh-grade teacher, said, "I know I'm not always a good listener. Sometimes I just go off on my own tack, whether or not anyone else is with me. There are some really good listeners in the group—I've been noticing. I don't promise that I'll improve, but I don't mind if people tell me to shut up."

There was more laughter, and I was really glad that Larry had the courage to say this. I think some other participants are intimidated by what they perceive as his more sophisticated knowledge. I'm hoping to help Larry not only in listening to others but in learning that he actually might learn something from some of the lower-grade teachers.

At this point, I asked if there were other ideas about working together that anyone wanted to discuss. Lynda said, "I don't like being so tied to an agenda. A lot of times we're having a good discussion and we have to stop to do the next thing. I'd like the timing to be more flexible."

I was concerned about Lynda's comment because I'd noticed in the last session that she was very active in the small-group discussion but tended to move the discussion off-track—bringing in particular teaching concerns of her own, rather than focusing on the student thinking in the cases. I decided not to answer this directly, but to ask what others had to say about this issue. Nancy was nodding and said, "Sometimes things move too fast for me and I'd like to slow down and spend more time."

Annie contributed, "It seems to me that there's always more to talk about, but I wouldn't want to give up doing the math for discussing the cases or give up the cases to do the math."

Donald said, "I'm actually not sure what I need to spend time on—I don't feel like I know enough yet about data to make that decision. I might feel differently after a few more sessions, but right now it's OK with me to let Maxine decide how to balance things."

Judith then added, "There have been times when I didn't want to move on. It seems like the more I know, the more there is to talk about, but I also know I'll never get *there* because there is no *there*."

"And there's so much to get through," finished Carolyn.

As I brought the conversation to a close, I was still worried about Lynda's stance and also wondered about Carolyn's final remark. Does she feel that the point of this course is to "get through" a certain amount of material? Some of the other remarks had brought some balance to the discussion, but I also wanted to acknowledge that it was important for me, as a teacher, to think hard about the balance between my agenda and theirs. I told them, "This is something, as a teacher, I struggle with all the time. I see really important conversations happening in one small group or in the whole group, but I also have an overview of learning goals for the course, so I have to think hard about the trade-offs of continuing to dig into an idea or moving on. I also have a sense of how many of these ideas will keep coming around again in different contexts, so sometimes I make decisions based on what I know about the course as a whole." I reminded them that they could use the exit cards to continue to let me know their thoughts on these issues.

Case discussion: Students' thinking about categorical data

As small groups got to work, I reminded them that they had worked with categorical data themselves in the first session with the question, *With what well-known person would you like to have a conversation?* I suggested that they keep that experience in the back of their minds as they discussed the cases.

I also pointed out that this is a different format for a case discussion than we had used previously, and that each group would be producing a piece of writing within the next half-hour. After everyone read through the handout, Ellen asked, "What do you mean by a mathematical idea?" Everyone laughed (including Ellen), but I could tell that the group was nervous about this. I had actually thought about this in advance so I had an example ready from their previous work. I reminded them that in the first session, a question had come up about whether to count duplicate responses in their data set. The "mathematical idea" here was about what each piece of data represented and how what should be counted relates to the purpose of the investigation. But then I added, "Don't get too hung up on what a mathematical idea is. If you think students are considering or using an idea about the data that strikes you as important, that's worth writing about."

The group interactions were very lively; this writing task seemed to be helping the less vocal participants focus on student thinking. Quite a few groups were talking about Barbara's case 7 ["Favorite Color: Where Is the Math?"]. They remarked that on the first day, when students *saw* the graph being built, they were connecting the representation to the data as the data were being collected. Judith noted that for the teacher, the graph represented a set of data, but it was unclear what it represented for the students. She thought they may have been trying to remember what they had done the previous day rather than actually getting information from the graph. Paul wondered if students can be so focused on the personal nature of the data that they aren't thinking about the question they are trying to answer—he said this could happen just as well for middle school students as for kindergartners!

Although it was difficult for most participants to name the mathematical ideas they noticed in the cases, the struggle to do so seemed worthwhile. They wrote about two major points:

1. The purpose of categories and how they provide information.

    Regina's group wrote:

    > In Maura's case, it made sense to group some responses into a more general category. "Pool" was more useful than the specific pools.

Helen's group wrote:

> We discussed the difference between starting with categories or having open-ended questions in "Mummy's Curse." Once the categories exist, they cannot be ignored. Like on a birthday graph, the class can't ignore months where there are no birthdays.

2. How to represent data so that it can be interpreted accurately.

Paul's group wrote about Rosemary's case 8:

> Initially students didn't think size of representation mattered; they felt only the number mattered.

And Marilyn's group focused on Beverly's case 9:

> All categories had to be labeled in order for others to understand their data. The teacher asked a key question, "What would happen if someone else wanted to find out about our class? What do you think they could tell from our survey?"

I was pleased that in all of the writing, the groups cited specific evidence from the cases, quoting both students and teacher.

Math activity: Describing numerical data

After the break, I asked participants to sit in the new groups I had posted for the math activity. Although everyone had worked with representing numerical data in the *How many years have you been teaching?* activity, there still remained a range of experience and confidence about working with data. I thought a few participants would find it difficult to create a data representation on their own, so I gave them the option of creating a graph individually or in pairs. I knew that the homework would give me a chance to see each participant's individual work.

Paul, Carolyn, Marilyn, and Diana were looking at the three graphs they had made. Paul had worked on his own, while Carolyn and Marilyn, working together, and Diana, working by herself, had drawn similar line plots. Their work is shown on the following page. At first, this small group had a hard time comparing the two kinds of graphs. It took Carolyn, Marilyn, and Diana a while to orient themselves to how Paul's graph was showing the data. I was tempted to help, but decided to listen to how Paul would explain his work.

After a little confusion, he pointed to a single point on his graph and said, "See, this dot is the height of Student F. If you go down from the dot, you hit the F—that tells you the student—and if you go over here [*he moved his finger horizontally to the left*], you hit 58—that's the height."

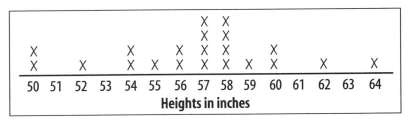

Carolyn, Marilyn, and Diana drew line plots like this one.

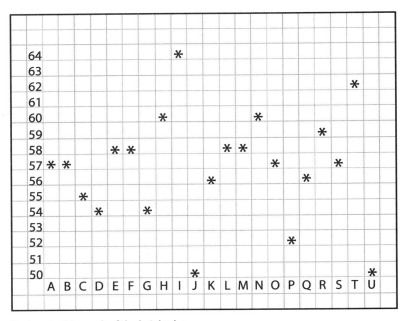

Paul made this graph of the height data.

I suggested that Paul demonstrate this again, using a different dot, which he did. Then Marilyn said, "Oh, I get it! The trouble is, it's the opposite from ours—the heights go up and the students go across." Others nodded and seemed satisfied with Marilyn's explanation.

I thought that the different orientations of the axes were part of what they had a hard time sorting out, but I wasn't sure whether they were also noticing that Paul's representation showed the values of individual cases (a case value plot), while the other graphs showed frequency. I said, "So on Paul's graph, what does a dot represent?"

Carolyn said, "It's the height of one student, like this one is student A and this one is student B. If the dot is higher [*she gestured to the top of the graph*], that means the student is taller."

"Then what does an X mean on this graph?" I asked, indicating Carolyn and Marilyn's line plot.

Diana explained, "It's also one student's height, but you don't see the whole height. You know it's 52 inches because it's in the 52 column."

Marilyn, who teaches kindergarten, said, "I think my students would see it better on Paul's graph."

Paul added, "But it might be better to have the actual names of the students."

This felt like a stopping point in their conversation, and I was starting to wonder if they were happy with a conclusion that a case value plot was "best," when Diana said, "In the line plot, I can see a shape to the data. I can't really see a shape in the other one."

Paul asked, "What do you mean by a shape?"

Diana responded, "Well, I can see a clump in the middle, like around 56 to 58. I can't see that in Paul's."

Carolyn said, "In Paul's, you can tell who is 56 and who is 57, but you can't see how they group together."

There was silence for a moment, then Marilyn said, "But you could change Paul's so they'd be in order."

I asked, "How would you do that?"

Marilyn said, "Well you'd put them in order first, so if 50 is the shortest, you'd put the 50's first, then the 51's, then the 52's, and you'd keep going."

Diana said, "But I still don't think you'd be able to see the clumps." I left them as they were starting to sketch what that representation would look like, reminding them to write down some statements that described the data.

One of the other groups also had both frequency and case value representations and had been able to sort out for themselves some of the differences between them. I considered bringing up this issue in the whole group, but I also knew that the cases for Session 4 would focus on this idea again, so I decided to hold off. However, I made a mental note to make sure that the participants who had already considered these two kinds of representations be scattered through the small groups for next session's case discussion.

When I stopped by the next group, Donald, Ellen, Rosa, and Traci were trying to write their statements. Donald indicated that the range was from 50 to 64. Ellen noted that there was a clump between 54 and 60. Rosa suggested 57 and 58 as the clump she most readily saw. The group discussed how you decide where the clump is and the fact that different members of the group could be seeing different sections as "the clump." Donald asked me if there was a correct way to decide which clump they should use.

I said, "Let's take a look at one of the possible clumps—say, the 54 to 60 clump. What is that telling you about the data?" The group looked at me a little blankly, so after a moment's silence, I tried to make my question more specific. "If you wrote down, 'There's a clump between 54 and 60,' what would that communicate? Let's say someone doesn't have the graph right in front of them—what would they understand by that statement?

Rosa was counting and finally said, "Well, you could say that $\frac{16}{21}$ of the data fall between 54 and 60."

I asked, "So saying something about the proportion of the data in that clump would help? Is there a more familiar fraction you might use?"

Ellen said, "About $\frac{3}{4}$." At that point, I thought they were on the track of thinking about summarizing the data by using fractions, and I left them to work on their statements.

Math discussion: Finding the median

Toward the end of small-group time, I put line plots of both data sets up on the board and asked for a few sentences to describe them. I wrote these under each graph. Participants seemed pretty comfortable describing the range, clumps, the mode, and outliers. I pushed a little on using proportions—using the work from Rosa and Ellen's group on $\frac{3}{4}$ of the data as an example. I asked the group to quantify the clumps they had identified for the data on number of years in town, and participants volunteered that the clump from 0 to 6 included about half of the data, while the clump from 10 to 14 included an additional third of the data.

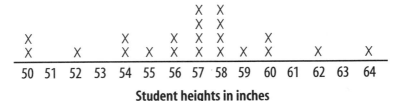

Student heights in inches

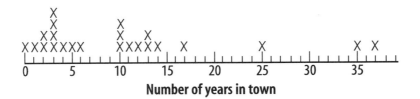

Number of years in town

I then asked for their thoughts about the graph made by fourth graders. Nancy said, "It just leaves out all the numbers that don't have any X's."

"So, is it an accurate representation of the data?" I asked.

Rosa said, "It's accurate, but you can't see the clumps."

Marilyn added, "You can still see that there are a lot of students at 57 and 58 inches."

Then Ellen asked, "But what if there were a lot at 62, but nothing at 59 or 60?" I stopped Ellen to sketch what she was describing, then asked her to continue. She continued, "So now it looks like there's a clump from 57 to 62, but there really isn't."

Carlos said, "When you leave out numbers, you can't see the gaps."

I decided to move on to the median. I introduced it this way: "One of the tools some of you used to summarize the data was proportion, expressed as fractions or percentages. Another tool you used is the range. Now we're going to begin our look at another set of tools for summarizing data—averages. A lot of you have been asking about averages since the beginning of the course, and when you say *average*, I think a lot of you are referring to the kind of average you get when you add up the values of all the pieces of data and divide by the number of pieces of data—like what you might do to calculate an average grade. There are actually several kinds of averages, and we're going to look more carefully at two of them in this course—the add-em-all-up-and-divide average, called the *mean* (officially the arithmetic mean, but we'll call it the mean), and another one called the *median*. We're going to learn how to find these averages, but, more important, we're going to work on making sense of them for ourselves. In other words, what is it that these averages tell us about the data?"

Melissa said, "There's another kind of average?"

And Karen said, "I thought there was just one kind of average—the add 'em up thing—and that those other ones—the median and mode—were just some other kind of thing." There were a lot of nods in the group, and I was glad Melissa had made her comment.

I explained that the median is the value of the middle piece of data in a data set and used the analogy of having students line up by heights—the height of the middle person would be the median value. I then asked participants to find the median in the data they had just plotted (student heights, and number of years in town). We worked through the process together, and then I showed them what to do with an even number of data points by adding one piece of data (at 61 inches) to the student heights graph.

I summarized: "So, the median of the student heights is 57 inches—half the data are less than or equal to 57 inches, and half the data are greater than or equal to 57 inches. And the median of the number of years in town is 10 years. So what does the median tell you about the number of years in town?"

Paul said, "Well, it's kind of misleading, because you'd think that half the people have lived there 10 years or less."

I responded, "And that's not true? What do other people think about that?"

Diana offered, "It is *true*. It's just that it's really 6 years or less."

I was concerned that we spend a little time sorting out what the median tells you and what it doesn't. When adults are learning about summary statistics, I notice that if a statistic doesn't tell everything about a data set, they tend to reject it as "misleading." A summary statistic, by its very nature, gives only certain information—it isn't providing information about all the features of the data. I wanted to give the group some sense of what the median communicates, then let them work with it for a while, to get a feel for what a median represents and what other information provides a context for interpreting the median.

I said, "So Paul and Diana are saying that the median doesn't show you that there's a gap between 7 and 10 in the data on number of years in town. The median—or any average—certainly doesn't tell you everything about what the data look like. But let's try to see what the median *can* tell you by comparing these two data sets." I circled the following two statements under the student heights graph:

> The range is from 50 inches to 64 inches.
>
> The median is 57 inches—half the data are less than or equal to 57 inches and half the data are greater than or equal to 57 inches.

I also circled the comparable statements under the data for number of years in town. I posed the following problem: "Suppose this is all the information you have about the data. You know the median, and you know the minimum and maximum values for these two sets of data. That is often the case—we read about a median or a mean, but we don't see the actual data. What would you know about the data just from these three pieces of information—the lowest value, the highest value, and the median? Work on this with someone next to you."

After a few minutes, I asked for thoughts. Lynda offered, "For the heights, the median is right in the middle, so you'd think that the data were even."

Suzanne added, "You might think it was like a bell curve with the two halves being symmetrical."

I summarized, "So Lynda is saying even, and Suzanne is saying symmetrical. Both of you seem to be saying that about half the data are in the bottom half of the range and about half the data are in the top half of the range." I drew a number line representation to illustrate what they were saying:

Then I asked, "What about the data on number of years in town?"

Ellen said, "Well, Judith and I thought that there's more data in the first half. The rest of the data are more spread out." I knew that there weren't "more data in the first half," but I thought this would get clarified as we went on.

Melissa said, "The data are much more scrunched together in the bottom half of the graph. Then the rest of the data are spread all the way out to 35."

Annie added, "If you look at the median, it's really low in the range."

I asked, "So what does that tell you, if the median is really low in the range?"

Larry responded, "It means that there's as much data in those few numbers below the median as there are in the whole rest of the range." At that point, I drew another number line representation to illustrate what Larry was saying:

Then Melissa said, "If you didn't know the range, then you couldn't tell that. You'd know there was a middle, but you wouldn't know how far each half goes."

It seemed to me that we'd made a lot of progress. I closed the discussion by saying, "We need to remember that averages and other statistics are summaries of the data. Over the next few sessions, we'll continue thinking about what information we can get from these summaries—how they are useful and what other information helps us interpret them."

Exit-card responses

I was glad that I had used an open-ended question for this exit card: "What are you learning about collecting, representing, and analyzing data? What are your questions?" The responses, which are very diverse, gave me a good sense of the issues on participants' minds—including things that have come up in class and others that haven't. Some people seem to be getting more comfortable with looking at data—thinking about the "big picture." And quite a few participants talked about how they are using their own experience in the seminar to think about the learning of their students. I was pleased that Larry is seeing implications for his seventh graders. He wrote:

> I think the experience that we are enjoying in this class is, how do we
> formulate questions, conduct surveys/gather information, and
> represent that data in useful ways. I personally would like my
> seventh graders to ponder these same sorts of questions. Rather than

just asking my kids to find the mean, etc., I'd like to ask them to consider how they should phrase a question, or what choices they should allow for answers, or what type of graph they should choose to best illustrate their findings.

Suzanne raised an important question:

I am still a bit confused about the median. Why is it important? Is there a name for the middle of the range? Or is it just middle of the range? What does that number tell you that's different from what the median tells you?

In my experience, it takes a while for both students and adults to work out why the middle of the range doesn't tell you how the data are distributed over that range. In retrospect, I'm surprised that this issue didn't come up explicitly today, but I think that may be because I was really pushing the whole-group discussion to focus on finding and comparing the medians in the two data sets. I'll need to slow down and allow time for participants to work through their ideas and confusions on their own during next session's math activity.

Comments about our discussion of how we are working together as a group were generally positive. Even though the group has been working pretty well together, this discussion is always important in affirming the diversity in the group and giving everyone a chance to reflect on how to create a supportive environment for learning. Regina commented, "It helped you see that each member is an integral part of the group, even when they are quiet or outspoken." And Annie wrote, "The discussion of our group work made me think about what I do in the groups and why I do it."

Responding to the Third Homework

October 25

In this homework, teachers wrote about how the seminar is going for them and what is on their mind about student thinking and about the math content of our work. Some of the participants still see the students in the cases as somehow different from their own; they seem to believe some kind of magic has brought these students to be critical thinkers. For example, Judith wrote:

I have been surprised by the level of critical thinking that some of the students in the cases show. The fact that they are actually questioning the data questions, as in the "Blue Jeans/Milk with Breakfast" case, is wonderful to see. My students don't even take the time to think about my questions—they just answer them. It's especially intriguing to see the young ages of these students with highly developed thinking skills. First graders are questioning and carefully responding better than my own third graders do! How have these ideas been developed so quickly and at such a young age?

To comments such as these, I wrote back about taking time to work on these activities over several months and giving students the time to develop a sense of data analysis as a process that results in information they can use to describe their world or to make decisions. I used Beverly's two cases—one from November and the other describing events in January and May—as an example of developing an idea (in this case, the need for developing a set of categories that reflects important differences among responses) over the whole school year.

I am still concerned about a couple of participants who don't seem to put much effort into the course work. Lynda's was one of the more cryptic responses. In answer to the first question, she wrote:

> I am enjoying the class and look forward to coming each time.

The rest of her responses were also short and vague. For example, in response to the fourth question, focused on what you are learning about, she wrote:

> I love working with data and finding different ways to interpret it.
> I would like to be able to use data collecting more extensively across
> the curriculum. It can be a valuable tool in teaching important
> thinking skills.

Lynda spends a lot of time in class telling me how wonderful it is, but I don't see her engaging herself intellectually in the content of the course. Responding to this kind of homework that shows so little effort is difficult for me because there is little of substance for me to grab onto. I decided that, since we are almost halfway through the course, I needed to be direct with Lynda about her work.

> Dear Lynda,
>
> I'm glad to know that you are enjoying the seminar and that you
> are looking for ways to integrate data collection into your classroom.
> In the portfolio writing assignments, I'd like you to try to write more
> specifically about your own ideas and the ideas of your students. Part
> of the work in this course is for everyone to really think hard about
> how students develop their ideas. Another part is to think hard about
> the math ourselves.
>
> Most of us didn't have a chance to do a lot of math work when we
> were preparing to be teachers, and sometimes the math we did take
> turned us away from math rather than drawing us in. I know it may
> feel unfamiliar, but in this course, I'd like to encourage you to write

more about what you are learning, what you are seeing in your students, what is confusing, and so forth. Using examples from your own thinking, from the cases, or from your students' work can really help explain these ideas. If you can write more about the specifics of your work, I can be more helpful in my written responses to you. Let me know if you want to talk further about any of this. I look forward to reading and responding to your next written assignments.

Maxine

Maxine's Journal

October 28

I knew that today's session was quite packed, and I wanted to make sure we had enough time for all three activities. I listed the names for small groups on the board and got them started at 4:00 P.M., even though a few weren't there yet.

Sharing pilot data

Participants were very eager to share their pilot questions and data. As I circulated, I noticed a lot of excitement and intensity. Some groups were using the study as an opportunity to look at an issue in their school. For example, one group had decided to find out about the incidence of asthma in the school and how it affected attendance. Another group was looking at the connection between the amount of reading at home and reading proficiency levels.

Other groups were using questions similar to the ones we had used for the surveys we did in class. Paul, Donald, and Helen were investigating how many hours teachers spend each week reading for pleasure. A few individuals expressed concern that the question their group had chosen wasn't "important" enough. For example, Judith and Melissa were looking at whether first graders can jump higher than kindergarten students. Judith said sheepishly, "It's kind of a silly question, isn't it?" I reassured her that it's not realistic for participants to come up with earth-shattering data in the short period of the seminar. What's important is learning about how to collect, represent, and describe real data, to learn what the *process* of data collection and analysis is like.

From what I heard, almost everyone had found that the question they had formulated, or the design they had used to collect data, was inadequate in some way. Respondents misinterpreted their question, or they found that they couldn't glean from the responses the information they had hoped for. Most groups said that the difficulty was finding a measurable question (a statistical question) that would give them good information. For example, the group focused on reading raised many questions about how to collect accurate data about the amount of reading at home—should they count the number of books read or time spent reading? Did they need to develop a way for students or parents to keep track over a certain number of weeks? How reliable would this information be? Participants were not reluctant to share with each other what had gone wrong. There was lots of laughter and acknowledgment that similar issues had come up for each project group.

I listened in, but decided not to be very active in these discussions. Participants were really listening to each other and trying to help, and I knew I'd have my chance to respond in writing to the work they handed in today. However, one group had collected categorical data. Ellen, Lynda, Marilyn, and Suzanne had put together data from two classrooms about which parents had attended their school's Open House. They had represented these data as a bar graph showing the number of families that did and didn't have a representative (22 *yes* and 24 *no*). When they convened as a group, they were already talking about the problem that these were categorical data.

I realized, as I listened, that there was a larger issue here. They had really been *interested* in information about which of their students' families attend school events so that they could think about how to involve those who don't attend, and they were feeling frustrated that they needed to change their idea in order to meet my requirements for the assignment. It reminded me of Natasha, in Andrea's case 6, who had bowed to pressure to change what she wanted to know. I wanted to validate their ideas and the fact that they had used data collection to find out something useful to their work, but I also wanted to be clear that they would need to find a way to collect numerical data for their project. I said that it was great that their pilot project had resulted in useful data for them, and that they could think about whether there were also some numerical data they could collect that would provide more insight. I reiterated that part of the purpose of the project was to give them an opportunity to use some of the tools we'd be learning about in class, such as averages, and that these tools couldn't be used with categorical data. I also said that they could certainly include some categorical data in their project, as long as they collected and analyzed some numerical data as well. They didn't seem very happy with my insistence that they find a way to work with numerical data, and I think I'll need to find a way to check in with them about their project work again.

Video and case discussion: What do the numbers mean?

After the 4-minute video excerpt from the "Pocket Data" clip, discussion began right away with a comment from Barbara. "I think the teacher's question—'What does that tell us?'—was too broad."

There is the tendency for some, in reading the cases or watching video, to assume that the students would "get it" if only the teacher would just ask the question correctly. I was concerned that Barbara's statement was heading us in that direction. To focus the discussion more directly on student thinking, I asked, "What's the idea the students are working on?"

Melissa said, "The numbers are confusing to them. They're trying to figure out, what are the X's for?"

Karen explained further, "They're figuring out that the number of X's in the 5 column means the number of people that have 5 pockets."

After a few more comments, I summarized, "Many of you are saying that the students are sorting out what the different numbers and symbols on the representation mean and how those are connected to the data they collected. Let's keep this idea in mind as we work on the cases." I hoped they would begin to get a sense of the complexity of developing and interpreting representations that coordinate values and frequencies.

As participants worked with the focus questions, several groups spent a lot of time trying to understand Figure 24 in Isabelle's case. One of the groups was making assumptions about what the graph showed without reading carefully, and I redirected them to look carefully at the text. In another group, participants were looking at the various representations in Isabelle's case in terms of which ones were "right" and which were "wrong." There seemed to be a lot of "oh my goodness, they're really mixed up," rather than discussion about the ideas these students were grappling with. Carolyn said, "Figure 22 is a mess—it makes no sense—there's no organization."

Sheila was taking a lot of time talking about how there should be labels on the graphs, and I decided to be fairly directive in moving them off this point. I said something like, "It's true that if we're presenting a graph to an audience, we need to have titles and labels that communicate clearly, but while students are working through issues of how to represent data, we can focus more on having them communicate what they are doing through verbal explanation. When you look at Figure 24, how do you think these students were making sense of the data? How were they showing number of people and number of teeth?"

One group had a very productive discussion of Denise's case. They referred to their own experience with the math activity in Session 3 as an example of the difficulty of understanding each other's representations. Paul remembered how others had a hard time understanding his graph, just as Cara and Tim had a hard time understanding Kenny's.

I had several objectives for the whole-group discussion. I knew that we should spend some time focusing on Figure 24 in Isabelle's case, because that representation had been difficult for so many participants to figure out. I also wanted to return to the difference between a case value graph and a graph showing frequency. But foremost, I wanted to keep the focus on how students need to think through which numbers represent the values of the data, which numbers represent frequencies, and how to develop and interpret representations that show both. I felt very challenged as a facilitator. There were a lot of complex issues here, and I was hoping to guide the discussion in a way that would be productive and focused enough for all participants.

I started by asking, "What is going on in Figure 24?" Ellen's group did a very good job of making this representation clear. After a few clarifying questions, I could see that most participants were following their explanation. Then I asked, "So how did this pair of students represent the two kinds of numbers in the data—the values of each piece of data and the frequency with which each value occurs? How did their approach differ from other students' representations?"

Suzanne said, "Well, they had separate stacks for the people and the teeth, so you have to know to look at the two stacks together."

Sheila observed, "It's really disorganized. You can't tell anything by just looking at it."

After a pause, Marilyn raised her hand and said, "It might look really disorganized to us, but I think Neil knew what each stack represented. We thought that they did a really good job taking all this information and putting it in some kind of order."

Regina added, "It took us a long time to figure it out, but once we did, we could see how Neil was thinking about it. And we noticed that there's even an order to most of it, except at the very beginning."

Quite a few people looked confused at this last statement, so I asked Regina to explain further. She held up her casebook and pointed out how the first pair on the right was about how many people had 2 teeth, the second pair was about how many people had 1 tooth, but after that the stacks went in order: how many people had 4 teeth, then 5 teeth, then 6 teeth, and so forth. This observation clearly surprised many in the group. I asked again, "How does this compare to how some of the other students represented value and frequency?"

At that point, Karen stopped me to ask me to clarify what I meant by *value* and *frequency*. I was glad that Karen had interrupted. I explained that, if I were giving this survey and asked a student, "How many teeth have you lost?" the number that student told me—4 teeth, for example—would be the *value* of that piece of data. When I finished my survey, the number of people who told me they'd lost 4 teeth would be the *frequency* with which that value occurred in my data set. I asked everyone to turn to Figure 20, and asked where we could see values and where we could see frequencies.

Larry said, "The values are 2, 3, 4, 5, along the left, and you can tell how many kids are at each value by counting the number of faces next to that value."

Carolyn added, "This is like a bar graph on its side—the length of the bar shows you how many kids lost each number of teeth."

"Actually, a graph that fits your description—like a bar graph or a line plot—is called a frequency distribution," I explained. "It shows the frequency of each value—how often each value occurs—in order of the values."

I was getting worried that we weren't really focusing on the ideas the students were thinking about in the case—how they were grappling with these two different kinds of numbers—so I decided to make my next question more specific: "How did the students who represented their work in Figure 22 or Figure 23 think about value and frequency?"

Barbara said, "Our group spent a long time thinking about Figure 22. At first, we just thought it was messy. There are numbers all over the place, but after a while we decided that it's really organized." I had everyone turn to Figure 22 and asked Barbara's group to explain further what they saw in this representation. Barbara went on, "Well, there's a box for each student that has the student's name, the number of teeth, and a picture of the number of teeth."

Nancy added, "And they're in order, so that first there's all the zeros, then the twos, then the fours. It's not really a—what did you call it?"

I said, "A frequency distribution."

"Yeah—one of those [*people laughed here*]. But you can still see that there are a lot of twos and a lot of sevens."

This comment was particularly interesting coming from Nancy, who often used her special-education lens to focus on students' use of language and had a harder time connecting with students' mathematical thinking. Here, she was really making sense of what she might have interpreted as disordered.

I said, "So even though they haven't put all the twos together in one bar the way Seth, Tracy, and Nikolai did for Figure 20, they've found a way to begin to show frequency. What about Figure 23?"

Paul said, "This one is kind of like Kenny's graph of the families. Each stack is one person."

Carlos noted, "But with Kenny's graph, you can't have a family with no people in it. With teeth, there could be kids with no teeth lost, and you wouldn't be able to see that in Figure 23."

Diana pointed out that you could "see" the frequencies in Figure 23, "because the stacks are in order, so all the twos are next to each other."

Larry then said, "But that's not true for Kenny's. His stacks of X's aren't in order, so it's hard to compare."

Ellen said, "I think with some discussion about what they could see in their graphs, Kenny might figure out that it would help to put them in order."

The group was starting to look a little glazed, so I concluded, "You're pointing out that thinking about *order* may be an important step in students' thinking about organizing data so that you can see both the values and the frequencies."

Math activity: Median as a tool in data description

We had about 15 minutes left to work on the math activity, which could be finished up for homework. As groups worked on representing the "Lost Teeth Data," I noticed that there was some difficulty in interpreting the table in order to construct a line plot. Participants weren't used to seeing frequencies expressed as numbers in a table. I was glad we could spend some time on this in class so that everyone understood how to interpret the table before they worked by themselves at home.

Responding to the Fourth Homework
November 1

For their work on the commute-to-school assignment, many participants were describing the data clearly and more fully than they had in the preseminar assignment. They seemed to be getting the hang of looking at the overall shape of the data. Many were comfortably using fractions, percentages, clumps, and median to describe the data.

Quite a few participants seemed to have some understanding of what the median showed about these data—that the lower half of the data are closer together, while the upper half are more spread out. However, some participants, while they described the overall picture of the data well, simply located the median but didn't use it in their description. For example, Ellen wrote:

> The range of times lies between 5 and 75—a range of 70 minutes. More than half of the data lie between 5 and 20 minutes. More than 75 percent ($\frac{16}{20}$) lie between 5 and 35 minutes. All but one of the travel times is under 50 minutes. The median is 20. I'm glad to see that most teachers spend 35 or less minutes commuting to work!

Since many of the participants' graphs and statements were similar, I decided to write a group response to this assignment. In part 4 of my response, I raised an issue that was brought up by one participant's graph. Barbara, who has been telling me since the beginning of the course how math phobic she is, was the only person to think about grouping the values by using intervals on the *x*-axis of her graph. I wanted to reinforce the thinking she had done and also bring this up as an issue for the group, even though we may not spend time on this in class. When I hand back the responses, I'll draw attention to this section. There were two examples of line graphs being used, inappropriately, for these data, so I decided that I would address this representational issue directly in the next session. Here is my response:

How long does it take us to commute from home to school?

Since there were many similarities among your work, I am not writing individual responses. However, I thought you might like to see the ways in which various class members described the important features of the data. I've selected below some statements and issues from your work that I thought were useful in describing these data.

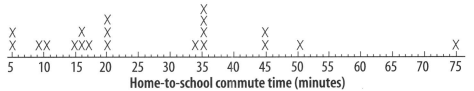

Home-to-school commute time (minutes)

1. Statements that capture the "big picture" of the data:

    ■ Half of the people take 20 minutes or less to get to work.

    ■ More than 75 percent [of the data] lie between 5 and 35 minutes.

    ■ Most people, or 80 percent, in the class commute to work in 35 minutes or less. 20 percent of those surveyed have a travel time of 45 minutes or more.

    ■ It's that 20–35 gap that "talks."

2. Statements about how the data are spread around the center:

    ■ The range of the first 10 people was 15 minutes. The range of the second 10 was 55 minutes.

    ■ The data below the median (20) are squished together. On the right side of the median, the data are more spread out.

    ■ This set of data is not symmetrically spread around the median. If it were, our median would somewhat reflect the middle of our range, about 35. It is really important to keep the middle piece of data (median) distinguished from midrange.

3. Statements about what values were unusual in this data set:

    ■ Only one person took more than 50 minutes to travel.

    ■ The outliers are important to look at if I was taking the mean because the outliers would affect the data outcome or the interpretation of the data.

4. Issues of representation:

Instead of quoting from your work, I'd like to raise an issue for you to think about. In representing these data, what are the advantages in showing every individual value, as in the line plot above? What are the advantages to grouping the data in intervals, as in this bar graph?

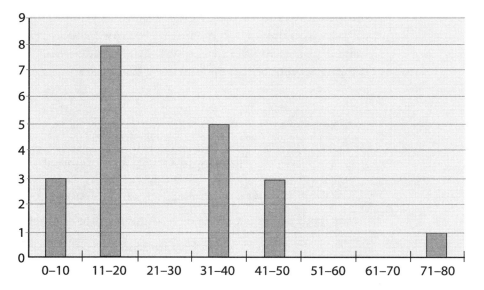

Each is a reasonable representation of the data. What aspects of the data does each highlight? What aspects of the data are harder to see in each? As one person pointed out about the first kind of representation, "Because the range is so spread out, the graph is very flat." In representation, there is a tension between showing all the individual values and showing a good summary of the data.

5. Interpretations of the data:

   ■ Eleven people are 20 minutes and below away from school: I hypothesize that they all live in the city.

   ■ Many people live close to their place of employment.

   ■ I'll bet that half live close to or in the town where they teach while half live outside the area where they teach.

6. Further questions you raised:

   ■ Do these all represent driving time? Are some people walking or making stops on the way?

   ■ Did everyone calculate one-way time? Does the value at 75 minutes represent one way or both ways?

   ■ How would the data look if grouped by school?

Data project pilot studies

I also wrote responses to each group's pilot of their data investigation. Larry, Rosa, Carlos, and Barbara were very enthusiastic about their study of asthma at their school. For their pilot they had surveyed the parents of one third-grade class. They asked: (1) Does your child have asthma? (2) How many people live in your household? (3) How many people in the household have asthma? (4) How many days of school did your child miss because of asthma? They had also collected a great deal of background information and had found that the urban area where their students reside had one of the highest numbers of hospitalization for asthma in the state.

The work they handed in included a summary of this background information, a summary of their pilot survey, and three graphs, two of which are shown below.

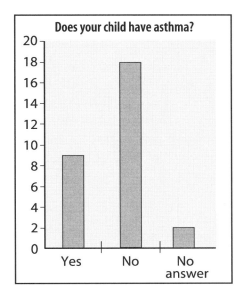
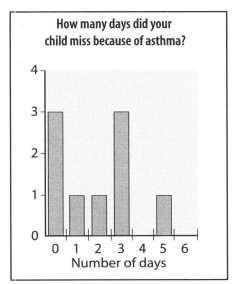

Dear Larry, Rosa, Carlos, and Barbara,

What I find particularly interesting about this study is that you are looking at an issue that affects many families in your school and gathering data that may both help you decide on a course of action and provide evidence to convince others that this action will be useful.

From what I understand, you first want to find out the incidence of asthma among families in your school. Your pilot study shows that $\frac{2}{3}$ of families you surveyed have asthma in the family. So one question you now have is: What is the incidence of asthma in the whole school? You have the sense that it might be this high in the whole school, but don't yet have enough evidence. In order to answer this question, you don't necessarily need to survey ALL families in the school. In this kind of situation, data are often gathered from a sample. Your pilot sample is probably too small (and only represents one grade), but you could decide to gather information from a larger sample rather than from all students.

You are also interested in how many students in your school actually have asthma. In your sample, at least 9 out of 29 have asthma—about $\frac{1}{3}$ of the students in that class. I was surprised and interested that the incidence is that high. So, again, the next question would be: Is the incidence of asthma that high across the school?

You pointed out in your discussion that the number of absences due to asthma was reported by parents and might not be accurate, so if you could use actual attendance records, you would have a better chance of accuracy. However, if that's not possible, I wouldn't discount parents' reports. They still can give you important information; you just have to report clearly that the data are from parents' recollections, not from school records, and know that when you are interpreting the data, there is some possibility that the numbers are either inflated or underreported. I am also wondering about the phrase "because of asthma." Is it always clear whether an illness or absence is asthma-related? It would be simpler to compare the number of absences of students with and without asthma without trying to determine which absences are asthma-related; overall, are absences of students with asthma higher? This question would also work to satisfy my requirement that you collect some numerical data and compare two groups.

So, as I see it, you have three possible questions from your pilot data to pursue as you look at the whole school:

- In how many families does asthma occur at all?

- How many students in the school have asthma?

- Do students with asthma have higher absences as a group than students without asthma?

Again, all three questions could be pursued with a larger sample rather than the whole school to make your investigation more manageable.

Maxine

Another group is studying home reading habits of students in their school. They started out with a broad question of interest and then struggled to formulate a question that could be studied. In part, their report read:

The literacy program at our school prompted our interest in whether there is a connection between literary proficiency and reading at home. Formulating the question was difficult. We started out wanting to ask, "How many books do you read?" But what is a book? Should poems count? *Harry Potter* will take longer to read than *Green Eggs and Ham*. We finally decided on the following question, "How long do I read or does somebody read to me at home in a week?"

We decided to use a whole week instead of school days only. The amount a student reads on the weekend is an important piece to consider. To collect the data, we broke the information down into a daily tally so it would be easier for students or their parent to keep track. They were asked to keep a log, which we supplied. Some questions arose as we began to collect the data: Are we pushing the data in a certain direction? Does a survey push results to occur? Will kids falsify data out of fear? We had a 40 percent return on our pilot. We would hope this would improve in our actual study.

Dear Carolyn, Regina, Nancy, and Sheila,

You did some great thinking about how to formulate your question. This is exactly what statisticians do—they start with a broad question like you did with *Is there a connection between literacy proficiency and reading at home?* Then they have to find a statistical question (or set of questions) that it is possible to investigate directly and that will give them some information about their original question. You really struggled with how to do that, realized that "how many books" was problematic, and settled on what seems to me to be a question that has a good chance of getting you some good data. I very much like your idea of using the log. Using the log, even if imperfect, certainly gives you a better chance at getting reasonably accurate data than simply asking students (or parents) to remember.

Your question about whether a survey pushes results to occur (or pushes students to give a false report) is right on the mark. Of course, in this case, pushing students to read more would be a good result! The more important question for you is exactly the one you seem to be asking: Do the returned logs represent some particular characteristic, for example, students who *do* spend time reading at home, while the unreturned logs represent students who don't read at home? One feature of your data that is striking is that no student who returned a log reported reading 0–29 minutes, so that does make you wonder whether those who don't read at home don't want to report that. It would be interesting to think about whether there is any way you could follow up that might give you some hint about whether this is true or not.

Your graph is very clear and informative. You made good decisions about choosing the subranges for values along the bottom of the graph. Clearly, with such a large range, you need a scale that groups the values, as you have done. Thirty-minute intervals seem to work well with these data to give an overall picture of the data. As you collect more data, you may want to play around with different intervals to see how best to represent the data; for example, would it be clearer or not as clear to show hours instead of half-hours? Let me know if I can help as you proceed.

Maxine

Maxine's Journal

November 4

Since last week, I received an e-mail from the group that had been having a hard time finding a question they wanted to pursue that used numerical data. Their note read:

> The four of us met yesterday to talk about our project. We came up with an idea to pursue, but I wanted to e-mail it to you before class to get any suggestions you might have. At our school we have a support team to help students who are having trouble being in the classroom. The support team keeps a daily log of every time they have such an interaction with students. We're thinking of talking to the members of the support team to see what information they might find valuable, and we are planning to look at the log to see what ideas might come out of it. We had thought of a few possibilities: Looking at the number of times a particular student visited with the support team, comparing which grade level had the most visits, etc. Do you have any thoughts about this? Ways to direct our thinking? Possible complications or traps we might fall into? Thanks!

This group seems really determined to investigate a meaningful question that might have some impact on issues at their school. I found their note pretty challenging. Because they are not choosing a simple question, but rather identifying an area of concern and then trying to find a question they can pursue, they are having difficulty finding a researchable question. Yet by doing this, they are really dealing with the complexity that has to be confronted in statistical research. I need to help them make their job manageable for this course while still respecting their desire to take on a meaningful project.

I wrote back to the team, suggesting that they look at the data on how many times per week (or other appropriate period of time) each student has an interaction. This would allow them to see how many students have no interactions, how many have 1 interaction, how many have 2, 3, etc., in that time period. Then they might do some comparing—among grades, among different days of the week, among students who have been at the school for different amounts of time, among different time periods. They might then be able to answer questions such as: Do interactions with the support team decrease as the year goes on? Are there differences between students who have been in the school less than a year and students who have been in the school longer? Are there differences among grade levels?

Sharing homework: Curriculum materials review

This activity gives participants a chance to connect what they have been learning in the seminar to the use of curriculum materials in their classrooms. Too often, teachers give their students activities without having clear learning goals. Perhaps they assume that learning goals are automatically embodied in the sequence of the curriculum activities. I think of this close look at curriculum materials as practice in defining learning goals while planning for a classroom activity. Only with clear learning goals in mind can a teacher modify tasks to make them more accessible or more challenging to the students.

Because many of the teachers were already using one of the NSF-funded elementary curricula or were interested in learning about them, I had made several activities from these curricula available to the group. As it turned out, some teachers who had used a particular curriculum for several years were so familiar with the activities at their grade level that they felt they didn't get much out of the analysis. If I have such teachers again, I might suggest that they look at an activity from a *different* grade level in order to learn more about learning goals for grades that either precede or follow their own—although I'm not sure that even teachers experienced with a particular curriculum always stop and think about what they are looking for in their students' work. For example, Annie commented, "I have done this activity for the last couple of years, but it was good to go over it in depth, remembering to read everything as opposed to just skimming over it before class because you think you know it."

I noticed that some participants were excited to directly link the work they had been doing in the seminar to their classroom planning. A few who had thought that this course would be giving them activities to do with their students seemed almost relieved, as if this is what they had been waiting for.

Even though some participants said this hadn't been that valuable for them, the small-group discussions were pretty lively. When discussion flagged, I focused the group on what they'd be listening for as their students did the activity. Later, when I looked at the exit cards, I found that despite some grumbling, most participants seemed to have found the activity helpful.

Line plots vs. line graphs

I knew from the homework that there was some confusion about the differences between line graphs and frequency distributions. In this seminar, we don't really work with line graphs, which show the change of one variable in relation to change in another variable (e.g., temperature over time), but I wanted participants to know that these two kinds of representations show different kinds of data. Before turning to our math activity, I wanted to talk about how line graphs differ from the representations of frequency we've been looking at. I used the data from Figure 20 in Isabelle's case and sketched this graph.

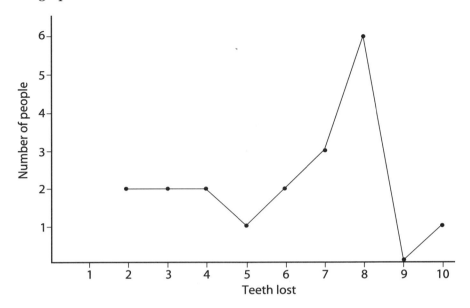

I decided to simply tell the group that this was not an appropriate graph for these data, explaining that lines on a line graph show a change from one value to another. For example, we can use a line graph to show temperature change. The high temperature today might be 55°, and tomorrow it might be 50°. The temperature has changed from 55° to 50°, *going through all the values in between*. The line between those two values shows that change. Here, we are not showing change from one column to the next—rather, we are showing how many people lost 2 teeth and how many lost 3 teeth next to each other so that they are easily compared. For example, the number of people who lost 7 teeth is three and the number of people who lost 8 teeth is six. One column has more data than the other, but nothing *changed* from three to six. I showed a quick sketch of a temperature graph showing daily high temperatures over a week and noted how the line between the high temperatures for Tuesday (45°) and Wednesday (39°) had to go through all the values between 45° and 39°, just as the actual temperature had to go through all those values as it fell.

Math activity: Discussion of 'lost teeth' data

To reorient everyone, I asked them to talk briefly with a partner about what they had noticed as they compared the Lost Teeth data sets they started last session and finished for homework. Then I asked what issues had come up for them.

Regina said that last session, her group had talked about how to treat the "don't know" data. When describing the data and talking about the range or finding the median, how could you include these?

Marilyn said, "We talked about that, too, and we decided that you couldn't really include them because they're not numbers."

Regina responded, "Right, but we were confused, because then isn't it misleading when you say the range is such-and-such or the median is such-and-such, because you're leaving those out?"

I asked what others thought about that. Karen said, "Couldn't you just report those separately? You could say how many kids didn't know, then you could report the range, or whatever, for the rest of the data."

I summarized at this point: "Actually, what you have here is a mixture of categorical and numerical data. You can put all the data in numerical order except for 'don't know,' which doesn't have a numerical value. So, in fact, you can do exactly what Karen is suggesting—report that a certain percentage of responses were 'don't know,' and then describe the shape of the rest of the data."

I asked what people had found out about the mode and median and what information those statistics conveyed about the data. Marilyn suggested that when the distribution is "pretty even," the median and mode will be similar. I asked her what she meant by "even" and she used her hand to show a bell-shaped curve, "You know, if a lot of the data are clumped in the middle."

I asked if anyone could point out where that was happening in our data, and Annie said that she thought the third-grade data were like that. "It's very spread out and kind of clumps around 8 and 9, so the mode's at 9 and so is the median."

Larry then offered that the range and median together are important—you get a lot more information from both than if you consider them in isolation. I asked if anyone could use an example from the data to demonstrate what Larry was saying. Judith responded, "For grade 3, the median is 9 teeth lost, but the range is from 2 to 19. If you just knew the median, you wouldn't know how spread out this can be for third graders. You might think that most third graders have lost around 9 teeth."

I pointed out that Judith was actually referring to the lowest and highest values—the extremes—not the range, which would tell us the distance between the extremes but not the actual values. I then asked if anyone else could talk about what we'd know about the grade 3 data if we knew the median and the extremes. Carolyn said that you'd know that at least half the students had lost between 2 and 9 teeth and that half the students had lost between 9 and 19 teeth.

Marilyn said, "About half the grade 3 students lost 8 to 10 teeth, and the median doesn't tell you that. It doesn't tell you how big a middle clump there is."

I wasn't quite satisfied with where we'd come in this discussion. I know it's difficult for participants to see the value of summary statistics when the data sets are small enough to see "at a glance." A second problem is that all three commonly used averages—mode, median, and mean—will be close to the same value in relatively symmetrical data sets, so it's difficult to see why the mode doesn't give you all the information you need. I wasn't sure if some participants were concluding that the median isn't useful at all because it doesn't tell you everything about the data, rather than developing an understanding of what such a statistic does and doesn't provide. So I decided to ask one more question.

"Suppose you knew only the medians for the four grade levels—suppose you read these in a report. Let's list them on the board." Participants told me what the medians were and I recorded them:

Kindergarten	0
Grade 1	5.5
Grade 2	8
Grade 3	9

I asked, "So, what would you know from this information?"

Paul said, "You can see that students have lost more teeth as they get older—which is what you'd expect, of course."

Diana added, "If you were a parent, you could see what a typical number of lost teeth is for a kid in the same grade as your kid."

There was silence for a minute, then Lynda raised her hand tentatively. "I don't know what you mean by 'typical,' because you still can't tell what's true for most students—a lot of first graders have lost between 7 and 10 teeth. If you looked at the 5.5, you'd expect less."

I turned her question back to the group: "So, Diana—or anyone else—what do you mean by 'typical' here? As Lynda points out, the median is not necessarily the number of teeth that most students have lost."

Again, there was some silence. I had the sense that the group was struggling with difficult ideas. I waited. Finally, Rosa volunteered, "Well, you do know that at least half the kids of that age have lost 5.5 teeth or more than that."

At this point I decided to summarize and move on. I knew that we'd come back to these ideas and expand them as we worked with box plots in the next session. I said, "The median gives you a cutoff point in the data, so you know that half the data are equal to or below it and half the data are equal to or above it. As data sets get larger—suppose we had a survey of several hundred students instead of just a handful—it becomes more difficult to view all the data. The median gives us one important summary statistic, one important landmark in the data set. If we know the lowest and highest values as well, we begin to get some sense of how the data extend on either side of the median, although we still don't know how that spread looks. Next time we're going to look at a representation that divides the data into four parts—quartiles—

instead of just into two parts, so we get an even better summary of how the data look. But now I'd like to turn to our work on a new kind of plot for today."

Math activity: Stem-and-leaf plots

As we looked at the stem-and-leaf plot for their commute time data, Barbara asked an interesting question: "So, you don't leave spaces for missing numbers in the leaves, but you do leave spaces in the stem?" I asked if anyone wanted to comment on that.

Marilyn said, "It's like leaving out a number on a line plot. It would look too squooshed together. It would seem like there was no gap, even if none was in the 40's, if you didn't have a line there for 40."

Donald asked, "Do you ever put commas to separate the numbers?"

I said that you didn't and added that it was almost as if you were using the ones digits to show the length of the "bar" rather than giving a list of individual values. Later, as I thought about this, I wondered if participants understood enough about why you wouldn't leave a gap for a missing value in the "leaves." This is really their first experience with a representation in which a bin or subrange is used.

Small-group work Participants were really fascinated with the two examples of stem-and-leaf plots. This representation was completely unfamiliar to all of them, except for James, who teaches grade 7 and has used curriculum materials that include work on stem-and-leaf and box plots. Seeing these examples from middle and high school curricula helped give the stem-and-leaf legitimacy in their eyes.

Although it seemed that the group had followed my demonstration of making stem-and-leaf plots, several groups had a lot of difficulty creating their own. Donald and Sheila were completely stuck. They couldn't find a way to translate the numbers they saw on the chart to a stem-and-leaf plot. I asked them if they thought that grouping by tens would be useful, or if they wanted to group by some other number. They decided to try fives, and I helped them set up the plot and worked through putting the first few pieces of data on the plot with them. They kept losing track of which values went on which line of the plot. In retrospect, I wish I had encouraged them to use tens first. I realized I'd been thinking too much about what made sense for the data and not enough about what made sense for them.

Barbara and Karen had plotted the data by tens easily, then tried using intervals of 5. They were curious about whether they could use some other grouping, and since they seemed to have the mechanics under control, I urged them to try a grouping by twos. I reminded them to take a little time to compare their plots to the bar graph.

Whole-group discussion Groups were still absorbed in their work when it was almost time to shift gears to work on the cases, so I had the group take a break, then brought them together for 10 minutes for a brief whole-group sharing.

Diana and Regina shared their work: "When we used fives, it was compact. We could see how the data were grouped. We could see that the third grade was shifted over from the first grade—in grade 1, most of the data were from 0 to 9, and in grade 3, most of the data were from 5 to 14."

```
        1st grade              3rd grade

    4  4  3  3  2  0  0 | 0 | 2
9 8 7  7  7  7  6  5  5 | • | 5 5 6 8 8 8 8 9 9 9 9 9
              2  0  0 | 1 | 0 0 2 3 3 4
                       | • | 6 9
                                    | 1 | 2 means 12 teeth
```

I asked the group to look at their stem-and-leaf plots and the bar graph of the same data. I wasn't surprised that quite a few participants said they found the bar graph to be much clearer than the stem-and-leaf plots. I knew from other experiences that when adults first encounter these new plots, they sometimes initially translate their discomfort with constructing the plots and the unfamiliarity of the plot itself into a sense that the plots are not as useful as more familiar representations. Participants made statements such as, "On the bar graph, you can see clearly that first grade has more at 7 and third grade has more at 8 and 9."

Barbara and Karen then said that they could see some aspects of the data on the stem-and-leaf that they couldn't see as well on the bar graph. They showed their plot that used intervals of 2. Karen said, "We could really see how the first-grade data clumped around 2 to 7 missing teeth—we couldn't really see that on the bar graph. The third-grade clump was 8 and 9." I quickly copied their plot onto the board and asked them to describe again what they could see.

```
    1st grade          3rd grade
          0  0 | 0 |
       3  3  2  2 | • | 2
       5  5  4  4 | • | 5 5
    7  7  7  6 | • | 6
          9  8 | • | 8 8 8 8 9 9 9 9 9
          0  0 | 1 | 0 0
             2 | • | 2 3 3
               | • | 4
               | • | 6
               | • | 9       | 1 | 3 means 13 teeth
```

Paul commented, "I really didn't notice how much of a clump there is in first grade from 2 to 7 with the bar graph—it's really clear in this plot."

Melissa said, "But isn't it kind of arbitrary? You can just keep making any groups you want, and it looks different each time."

I asked what others thought about Melissa's statement, and Annie said, "But you're still comparing the same thing—if you group the first grade by twos, you have to group the third grade in the same way."

Judith said, "It's starting to make sense to me. I can see what Barbara and Karen are saying, but I still don't think I have it completely straight. I have the feeling that there's a way to use these, but it doesn't feel comfortable yet."

I decided to leave the conversation here so that we would have enough time for the case discussion. I acknowledged Judith's comment and confirmed that it takes some experience to figure out when and how to use a representation like this one. I urged the group to keep playing around with the stem-and-leaf plot, reminding them that it was generally more useful when the data were even more spread out than the data we had been using for practice. I suggested that they consider trying this kind of plot with their project data, if it seemed useful.

Video and case discussion: Comparing groups

After the first video segment, I paused the tape and asked, "Why might the teacher ask students to think about differences in the range [in Lost Teeth data] at each grade level? What insight do you get into children's thinking as they talked about why the ranges would be different?" These questions seemed to open up some good discussion.

Melissa offered, "She might be wanting to get them beyond the individual numbers to focus on the kind of information that they are getting—seeing the big picture. Otherwise students often focus on who 'wins.'"

Rosa added, "They are thinking of more grades than their own. They are focusing on people other than themselves. The question forces them to look at numbers in sets more than individual points."

Nancy said, "That's what I was thinking. In my mind, the teacher was trying to get them to think about what the data really show us."

Barbara then referred back to the earlier video we saw, showing a second-grade class: "Like in that first video we saw about the pockets, the point is that the numbers are more than numbers. They mean something."

Karen brought up a different point. "I think she's trying to get them to focus on the numbers, what the data actually show, and not interpretation." Karen's idea provoked a lot of responses.

Paul said, "The teacher was asking them to think about why they would predict particular ranges, which *is* getting at interpretation in some way. "

Carolyn remarked, "It's really difficult to get kids and adults to look at the data and see what they really mean. In our district, we're looking at test data. And we see people jumping to their own particular interpretations. So there's this tension between what the data actually say and our interpretations of it."

Regina observed, "When you look at one data set, you're limited at what you can look at. As soon as you look at another data set, you begin to ask why. And that's the power of having more than one data set—it expands your reactions. You immediately start to compare it. The kids in the video only had their own experience and it was very personal. As soon as you get beyond that, you can really start to look at things."

I was pleased to hear the group focusing on two important points: helping students to base interpretations on careful analysis of the data, and the power of using data to compare groups. I brought this part of the conversation to a close by saying, "So you want to get to interpretation at some point, but it sounds as if you're saying that you want to make sure those interpretations are grounded in a careful description of the data."

After the video, I suggested that participants start off their small-group case discussions by talking about the final segment, considering what the students were noticing and not noticing about the data.

All the groups had a lively discussion about Evelyn's case 17, speculating about why students could describe the data in a more focused way when they compared two grades. Helen, Carlos, and Donald were typical. Helen suggested that there is something about structuring the graph for the kids, out of their view, that makes it harder for them to connect to the data (the teacher had created the graph at home and brought it back the next day). Carlos felt empathy for the teacher; he said she probably worked very hard on the graph and then must have been disappointed when the kids didn't seem to focus on the data. Donald, a kindergarten teacher, added that the interaction is so typical of kindergarten.

As they moved on to consider the second conversation in which the students compared the two groups, Donald said that it seemed counterintuitive that connecting the big picture across two groups would be easier than looking in detail at one thing. He said that he initially thought this would be especially true for younger students and wondered what would happen if he tried this in his own classroom. Helen suggested that maybe it was actually easier to compare two groups because it gave more of a purpose to saying something about the data. If you were just looking at one group, you might be thinking of all kinds of questions; when you compared two groups, you narrowed your focus about what question you were answering.

I asked, "What question do you think they were answering in the second conversation?" Carlos said it was something about what was similar and what was different. This idea of having a clearer purpose for describing the data was an important point to bring up in the whole-group discussion.

After about 25 minutes in small groups, I decided to pull the whole group together. To start the discussion, I asked, "What did you think about the role of comparison in these episodes? How did comparing two or more groups affect the way children viewed the data?"

Participants brought up several key points. Ellen, another kindergarten teacher, observed that when you compare two classes, you move away from the "individualness" of the data. She noted, "You're not just saying 'I picked purple.' You're looking at the bigger picture. And when you look at that other class, you're not saying, 'Chris liked purple and Cara liked yellow,' because you don't even know who picked what. You have to look at it as a whole."

There were many similar comments as we discussed the cases. Just as I thought we might be ready to bring the conversation to a close, Rosa brought up a different point: "Everything we read in this discussion—it looks like comparison is really important. But when we were looking at other cases, there were other issues that kids had to really understand about one data set, like in the pockets video, or Isabelle's 'lost teeth' case last week."

Nancy then added, "With my second graders, if you give them too many pieces of data, it can be confusing. So sometimes, you have to look at one piece at a time and build on it. When they don't know what you're looking at, it can become overwhelming. Like the pocket data, you have to think about how many pieces of information they can think about at one time."

Rosa had brought up an interesting issue that I thought was a worthwhile counterbalance to the enthusiasm for comparison. However, I wondered how Nancy, a special education teacher, had taken Rosa's comment. She often says that she needs to simplify for her students, and I'm concerned that she is quick to create activities in small steps which ensure success but don't push her students to investigate the ideas. Before ending the conversation, I wanted to at least challenge this notion that simplifying is always the way to go. So I ended the session by trying to sum up and leave them with a question.

"I'm hearing what some people might think is a contradiction in this discussion. A while back, some of you said that comparing groups in Evelyn's case actually helped students look at the big picture, even though it seems that it would be harder to look at two groups than one group. Then Rosa pointed out that there are some issues that students might need to work on with only one set of data because those ideas—like sorting out how some numbers refer to the values of the data and some numbers refer to frequencies—are complex in themselves. What do you think? Do we need to go for the more complex to push students' thinking, or do we need to make data sets simple enough so that students can manage them? I'm not expecting one, simple answer, but I think this is a teaching issue we can keep thinking about. Since you will all be doing an activity that involves comparison with your students for next time, we can continue this discussion once we have some more experiences to share."

Exit-card responses

This session felt packed with new learning, and I was curious to read the exit cards. I had posed two questions, one about the curriculum review assignment and one asking them to comment on their work with stem-and-leaf plots. I wasn't surprised to read that while some participants were intrigued by the stem-and-leaf plot, others couldn't see its value. For example, one participant wrote cryptically: "I didn't care for it. I feel it's confusing to the reader." However, all in all, participants seemed open to learning about new representations and using them to push their own thinking about describing data. Barbara wrote:

> I liked this way of graphing the data, especially for comparing two groups. In some ways, it makes the data clearer than a double bar graph. It is easier to see the clumps in stem-and-leaf plots when you are comparing two groups. I think children (those able to understand place value) could 'see' data even more accurately than sometimes comparing two separate graphs. We may use it for our data project.

Several teachers commented on how this experience connected to their students' learning. One observed:

> I taught sixth grade last year, and the middle school students seemed more willing to try something new than we are! I think as adults we're much more rigid in our thinking, much quicker to say 'this isn't good' or compare it to what we're used to. I don't feel comfortable with the stem-and-leaf, but I want to give it more of a chance.

Comments on the curriculum review were also somewhat mixed. There were a few who persisted in feeling that this "exercise" had been a waste of time, especially because they hadn't actually done the activity with their students. For example, Lynda wrote:

> No way! Was a waste of time to sit and do it as a homework project. We do all those things naturally. That's what teaching is.

Hmmm. I wonder if we *do* always think through the mathematics in a lesson naturally, even after many years of experience? Others in the group, however, had a different point of view. Karen's response was typical:

> It gave me a chance to look at the session carefully without the need to be ready to do it. I like finding the math in it. Discussing it with others brought up things I hadn't thought about. We don't always have time to really think through a lesson like this, and I think it's worthwhile to be forced to be more analytical.

Responding to the Fifth Homework

November 8

When I read over the curriculum review homework, I found that most of the participants had answered the three questions, carefully considering what they wanted students to get out of the activity. Since there was much overlap among the papers, I responded to the group as a whole, including a summary of their responses to each of the activities they had worked on. Some teachers had said that they wished they could hear what was going on in other groups, so I thought having a summary of each group's work would be useful. Here are my introductory comments.

Summary from the curriculum review assignments

For this assignment, I'm responding to the class as a whole, for two reasons: (1) There is a good deal of overlap among papers that analyzed the same activity, and (2) some of you expressed interest in knowing what was discussed in other groups about other grade levels. Although some of you felt that because you were so familiar with the activity you analyzed, the task provided no challenge, I found the papers as a whole gave a good sense of how a teacher defines learning goals and then keeps those goals in mind while seeing students do the activity. Your work illustrates how important the intention and reflection of the teacher is in using published materials.

After this introduction, I listed for each activity some excerpts from participants' papers, then wrote a paragraph summarizing the mathematical focus of the activity, as well as any issues raised in the set of papers.

Maxine's Journal

November 11

Sharing written homework: Student thinking

We began the session working in small groups to share the cases everyone had written. As I walked from group to group, I sensed a great deal of energy. Participants were eager to share the work they had done with their own students, and many expressed surprise, interest, and curiosity about what they had noticed. I heard quite a few comments that comparing two groups had led to more specific observations and discussion about the data than in past activities.

I noticed a couple of issues that I'll want to address in my responses to their work. Paul (who was late again—I decided to speak to him about this at break) hadn't understood what "compare two groups" meant. He had his fifth graders collect and represent data about their ages. In his group, he acknowledged that he was confused about what it meant to compare groups. He thought that having both 10- and 11-year-olds in the class qualified as "two groups." Because I had decided to put people in grade-level groups, Paul was with two other fifth-grade teachers, Annie and Melissa. This turned out to be helpful because he was able to hear about the ways their students had compared groups and to get some ideas for the future. Annie gently suggested, in a way that Paul seemed to hear, that gathering data in which the range of results was so small (everyone was either 10 or 11 years old) didn't offer much opportunity for analysis. Paul said that perhaps they could go on to comparing the heights of the 10-year-olds to the heights of the 11-year-olds.

In another group of fourth- and fifth-grade teachers, Regina had just finished describing the work her students had done in comparing their own travel times to school with the set of commute data for the teachers in our seminar.

Carlos then presented the work his fifth graders had done—graphing favorite colors for two grades in his school. Carlos thought it was interesting that the older children had fewer favorite colors than the younger children. Carlos had brought his students' graphs. They had represented each data set, then written statements about what they could see in the data. The graphs were very meticulous. The children obviously had worked hard on them— something Regina noted with envy. However, several of the children had used line graphs—connecting the tops of the bars representing each color with a line. Regina and Judith asked about the use of the line graphs, referring back to my brief discussion of line graphs in the last session. Carlos was somewhat defensive and said he was really pleased with what his children had done. He seemed to feel that the graphs looked like "real graphs," and I think this was important to him. Judith asked if the students had been given the opportunity to compare and discuss the representations they had used. Carlos said that he felt they had done enough with this activity and would be confused by considering other graphs. I think Carlos has done very little with data analysis in the past, and I am glad to see this beginning work. I want to encourage him to go further, but I'd also like to see his fifth graders work with data a little more complex than favorite colors—and to help him understand the difference between line graphs and frequency plots. I'll need to think carefully about how to respond to his writing.

As a transition to the case discussion, I pulled the whole group together and asked if there were any general comments they wanted to make about what they had noticed when their students compared data from two groups. Karen said that using a second data set helped her third graders describe more of the "big picture" of the data. They were very interested in finding differences between the groups, describing these differences, and interpreting them. Several others concurred that their students' interest had been sparked by comparing groups. Suzanne said that going to another class to collect data made her students feel like "real mathematicians"—like they were doing something important. Ellen added that she found that the questions she asked were critical in helping her students get beyond focusing on "who wins" to describing similarities and differences between the two groups. Finally, Larry contributed his observation that it had worked well to have his students make predictions before gathering the data; he mentioned getting this idea from the video we had seen in the last session. He said that his students really wanted to know how the data came out in order to see if their predictions were confirmed.

Small-group case discussion: Student ideas about average

As I prepared for this class, all four focus questions seemed important, and each raises a somewhat different issue. While I usually don't rush participants to get to all the focus questions, I decided that I would like the groups to touch on each of these. I told the group that we would be spending a full hour in small groups, and that they should spend no more than 15 minutes on each question so that they would have some time to discuss each one. I acknowledged that I often don't ask them to move on when they are having good discussions about a single question, but that I was asking them to handle these questions differently.

As discussions began, I got the impression that this had been a challenging set of cases for many participants. Rather than digging into the specific questions on their sheet, a couple of groups were talking in more general terms about their own confusion about average. For example, Karen spoke of being confused by the terms *mode*, *median*, and *mean*. She seemed to have ideas about the various kinds of measures—that one was about middle, one had to do with "most," and one was about adding up and dividing—but she couldn't keep straight which term was connected to which idea. I spent a minute with her group, briefly helping them get this straight, since it seemed to be distracting them from their work on the cases. Then I directed their attention to the first question and asked them to start making a list of the different students' definitions of average. I had to be fairly directive with another group as well. I mentioned to both groups that we would be spending more time working on ideas about averages as adults, but that I'd really like them to focus now on *students'* ideas about averages—that, in fact, this would be a route to clarifying their own ideas as well.

I kept the groups moving from question to question by reminding them to move on every 15 minutes or so. Although it was somewhat difficult, everybody was a good sport, and by the end of the small-group time, all the groups except one had spent some time on all four questions. I decided that we'd spend time as a whole group on questions 1 and 3—the first because it seemed to me that most groups were struggling to articulate the differences and similarities between "everyday" and "mathematical" ideas about average; the third because there was some real confusion about what Pat's method of finding the "middle" was and how it related to finding median.

Whole-group case discussion

I asked the group to tell me some of the "everyday" notions about average that they had noticed in the cases. They contributed several ideas, including *regular*, *usual*, *normal*, and *most*, which I wrote on easel paper under the heading, *Everyday Ideas about Average*. Then Barbara said that her group had thought some of the students were using a somewhat pejorative meaning for average: "When Lamont says, 'Somebody could be better than what most people can do,' and then what Jasmine says at line 48. It's not just that average is usual, but it's not as good to be average."

Larry concurred: "It's like no one wants to be average; everyone wants to be above average. No parent thinks their own child is average or regular or ordinary—their child is special."

Donald noted further that while C is considered an average grade, you're not very happy if you get a C. Participants suggested I write *just OK, but not better than OK* on our list.

I then wrote *Mathematical Ideas about Average* on the easel paper to start another list and asked what they had noticed about students' mathematical ideas about averages. I wasn't prepared for the complete silence and looks of discomfort. I waited for a while. Helen finally said, "Well, they're not saying anything about adding up numbers and then dividing!"

Everyone laughed, and that seemed to relieve the discomfort a bit. It also gave me a hint that despite the fact that we had talked about there being different kinds of averages, perhaps the "real average" was still, for many of them, the mean. I said, "So there's the kind of average Helen is referring to—the mean. We all learned the add-and-divide algorithm in school. But we've also talked about the median—another kind of average. And the mode is another average—another way to summarize a set of data, especially categorical data. Do you see in the students' thinking any beginning ideas of ways to find a number that summarizes a set of data in any of these ways?"

Rosa offered, "Well, we already have *most* on our list about everyday ideas, but isn't that really a mathematical idea, too?"

I asked if anyone could elaborate on this idea, and Ellen said that *most* was connected to the idea of mode.

When I pushed for other beginnings of mathematical ideas, Regina said she thought that in Isabelle's case, Neil's idea was the most mathematical. She cited line 69 where Neil was describing a number that would be in between *most* and *least*. Paul added that Neil's idea was connected to what the students in Suzanne's case did when they were finding a middle value. After a bit more discussion, during which I asked for examples from the other cases, our lists looked like this:

Everyday Ideas about Average	*Mathematical Ideas about Average*
regular, usual	what occurs most often
normal	middle of the extremes/middle of the range
most	
not as good	middle of all the values (median)

I then asked what I knew would be a difficult question, but I wanted to see if the group could grapple with it: "So what are the differences between the ideas we've written down under these two lists?" I asked everyone to talk to someone next to them about this question for a minute or two. After a couple of minutes, quite a few people seemed ready to contribute to the whole group. Here is part of the discussion that followed.

SUZANNE: What this makes me think is how complicated "average" is—it must be tough for kids. They come with these ideas about average that really aren't what we're talking about in math.

MAXINE:	So what are we talking about in math? What's the difference between the first list and the second list?
MARILYN:	The first list is more about people. It doesn't have to do with numbers.
MAXINE:	So couldn't we be talking about people when we give a mathematical average, say average heights or average time we watch television?
ANNIE:	It's that in the first list, you just look at one person and say, "Oh, that person can ride a bike or whatever, but she can't do fancy bike tricks," like that kid in Isabelle's episode said. So she's an average bike rider—she's just normal. But if you are making a mathematical average, you have to look at a whole group of people.
LARRY:	A mathematical average would be more precise—it's based on data. When you're using average like Marilyn said—like what's usual—you're just basing it on your intuition. You might be wrong.
DIANA:	But I don't think you're necessarily wrong when you're saying "average" in an everyday way. If you were saying, "I drive at an average speed," you might not know exactly what average is, but you know you don't drive way fast or way slow.
MAXINE:	And what would you base that judgment on?
DIANA:	Well, you see what goes on around you. You're driving along normally with traffic. You're not whizzing by everybody and you're not holding up the line.
MAXINE:	So Diana seems to be saying that while there are differences between these two lists, there are also some links. Some of the everyday notions are connected to some of the mathematical notions. Your example about traffic seems to have the idea about average being in between extremes, and averages also capture something about what's more typical of a group rather than what the extreme values are.

I noticed our *mathematical* list was missing any ideas that specifically connect to the mean—such as balancing, or "evening out." But I thought that these ideas would be coming out as we worked on the mathematics of the mean in Session 7 and the cases in Session 8. At this point, I decided to move on to question 3, since several of the small groups had been struggling with how Brynn's idea of middle differed from Pat's idea of middle [in Suzanne's case 22].

I asked the group first to describe Brynn's way of counting, then Pat's. Barbara described Brynn's way clearly and noted that she is finding the median; then Carolyn described Pat's way of counting. Donald added, "Pat is counting each value once. If there are duplicates, he doesn't count them. Brynn counts each height, even if some of them are the same."

I asked, "So how do Pat's and Brynn's methods differ?"

Nancy and several others raised their hands. Nancy isn't usually very confident in giving an opinion on mathematical ideas, so I called on her first. She said, "I'm not really sure, but it seems to me that when you're finding the median, you're counting every single piece of data, but if you use Pat's method, you're just counting the numbers." I asked for other comments and several others contributed their thoughts.

MELISSA:	If you use Pat's method, you're not that close to the real middle.
MAXINE:	And by "the real middle," you mean . . . ?
MELISSA:	The median.
SUZANNE:	I kind of see it. If you're just counting any place where there's some data, even if it's just one X, then you're not necessarily saying anything about where most of the data are.
MAXINE:	So Suzanne is saying something about the weight we give to each piece of data. When we find the median, each piece of data is counted as one. When we use Pat's method, one value at 19 gets counted as one, and all the values at 9 also get counted as one.
MELISSA:	It could come out the same, though, if the data set was pretty symmetrical—like it came out the same when Pat and Brynn did it.

I was afraid everyone was almost out of energy to think about these ideas further, but I felt Melissa was pointing out something important. I was also concerned that the teachers would end up with an overly simplistic conclusion that Pat was "wrong" and Brynn was "right." So I pushed the discussion a little further by saying, "Melissa is pointing out that sometimes—you're saying when the data are symmetrical—Pat's method would give you the same result as the median. In fact, it *did* give the same result in Suzanne's case. So, what about Pat's and Brynn's thinking? Are they thinking about important ideas?"

KAREN:	Well, they're doing more than thinking about just "the most." Our group was talking about how even though the most kids are in the group that's the tallest, they're not saying that the tallest kids are the average.

DONALD:	They're thinking about ideas about middle. Even if they have different methods, they're both thinking about middle.
SUZANNE:	And they're only third graders! It's like what happened in Alice's case [about temperatures], too—they need to be looking at all the data, not just doing some calculation to find the middle. Look how difficult it is for us to sort out all these ideas about which middle is which!

The group laughed, and I brought the discussion to a close.

Math activity: Box plots

It's always difficult to start something new toward the end of a class, but it turned out that being able to listen to a presentation was a welcome change of pace for participants. I still had to gear up and refocus *my* energy, though! I told the group that I'd be presenting the second type of data display that I had mentioned last time and then they'd get a chance to look at some examples and try to make one of their own as well.

I reminded them that the stem-and-leaf plot gave us a way to show all the values in a data set, that we could include a relatively large number of values, and that we could compare the shape of the data in two data sets. I said that the box plot—or box-and-whiskers—was a quite different kind of representation. It didn't show all values of the data, but was a summary representation built around the median. I mentioned that this type of display can be used for very large data sets, even much larger than what can be shown in a stem-and-leaf, and that box plots can also be used to compare any number of different groups.

I then introduced the five-number summary—the basis of the box plot. I asked if anyone had encountered the term *quartiles* and knew what it meant. Regina said that it had to do with quarters or 25 percent. Paul added that they sometimes got information about test scores in quartiles—so you'd know which students were in the lowest quarter, the second quarter, the third quarter, and the top quarter. I explained that a box plot requires us to divide the data into quarters, so we start by finding the median, then divide each half of the data in half again. I put up the stem-and-leaf plot of their commute-to-school data and together we used that to develop the five-number summary:

Lower extreme	5
Lower quartile	15.5
Median	20
Upper quartile	35
Upper extreme	75

Then I walked them through the steps for making a box plot for these data.

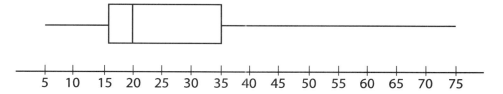

I asked the group to describe what they could see in this representation. I wasn't surprised that this was pretty difficult. At first, box plots aren't easy to interpret.

Judith said, "Well, you can tell that the median is at 20."

Suzanne said, "When you just put up the five numbers, I could understand where those numbers came from, but it's really hard for me to see what these shapes are."

I said, "Keep in mind that each of these boxes—to the right and left of the median—are 25 percent of the data. What can you say about this 25 percent?" I pointed to the box to the right of the median. Slowly, participants were able to describe what the range of the data was in each quartile. Then I asked, "So why is this quartile [the right side of the box] so much wider than this quartile [the left side of the box]?"

Ellen said, "I think . . . because on the left side there's a lot of data squished together, and on the right side, there's the same amount of data, but it's much more spread out."

I said, "Here's what's hard about learning to read box plots: It's easy to think that the width of each quartile is showing you *how many pieces* of data are in each chunk. But that's not what it shows. You have to remember that each chunk is *the same amount of data*. What the length of the line or the width of the box shows you is how spread out or how close together that 25 percent of the data is. A lot of you have observed that the median by itself doesn't give you an adequate picture of the data. That's exactly what a box plot is for—it gives you the median and then it gives you a summary of how the data are spread around the median."

I thought they should now turn to working with box plots themselves. Only through digging into several box plots would they get a feel for how to interpret this representation. They spent the rest of the session in small groups, looking at the examples of box plots and making their own box plot with the Lost Teeth data. Much of their discussion focused on sorting out what the width of the box or length of the whisker indicated. Several participants said that it was counterintuitive for them—that they kept thinking that a bigger box meant more data.

We didn't have time for a whole-group discussion, but I felt that the work in small groups needed to continue. Working closely with box plots themselves was the only way participants would come to understand this type of data display. And, I hoped, by using this representation, they would develop a better sense of how the median and interquartile range could be used to describe a set of data.

Exit-card responses

I asked the participants to comment both on their ideas about students' understanding about average and their own understanding of average. The exit cards confirmed my hunch that there was quite a bit of diversity in the group in their understanding of average. Several participants have a clear sense that the median doesn't tell you everything you would like to know. For example, Marilyn responded:

> The median isn't enough. The median tells you the middle but it doesn't give you a full indication of the range. It's a partial picture. You've got to know more.

Many of the teachers are grappling with their realization that using averages is much more complex than they once thought, both for themselves and for their students. As Judith wrote:

> Students in the cases are asking good questions and bringing up valid points about average. They seem to start out with a qualitative view, and it gradually evolves into a more complex quantitative one as more experiences are added. My question is: What are the experiences that really help them move along in developing a more "mathematical" view? When I learned about averages, it was just a formula, but I'm realizing how little I really understood about how an average works. I think students need lots of experiences with different data sets and especially comparing groups to learn about these ideas.

A few teachers are still focused mostly on average at a procedural level. They seem to be working so hard just to keep in mind how to find an average that they are not thinking about the nature and use of an average. Sheila wrote:

> I understand that the median is the middle number in a set of data when the numeric data are ordered from least to greatest. I also learned that where there is an even number of data, you take the number that is between the two numbers in the middle. Ta daaa!

However, given Sheila's self-proclaimed math phobia, I'm glad to hear her feeling confident.

Responding to the Sixth Homework

November 14

Having listened to Carlos's presentation of his students' work in the small group, I knew that there were several issues I wanted to address in my response. I wanted to affirm the fact that he'd taken an important step in doing some data work with his class. At the same time, I wanted to challenge him to think a little further about how his students might compare and analyze their representations, and I wanted to make a suggestion about moving beyond categorical data. He handed in copies of his students' work along with his written episode.

Carlos
November 9

The first thing my students did was to decide what they wanted to know about their class and the fourth-grade class. After some discussion they decided they wanted to know what was the color fifth and fourth graders like the most. They collected the data by asking all the fifth graders and fourth graders what their favorite color was. After that they tallied all the answers, and when they were done they did their graph. First they did a graph for each class. Second, they looked at the graph and wrote three statements about what they saw on the graph. These are some of the statements my students wrote:

1. I know that blue got more in the fifth grade.
2. I can see that almost no one likes green.
3. I know that they like red more than green.
4. The blue is the biggest because blue has 12.
5. The green is the smallest because green has only 1.
6. I know that the total number of students in the class is 23 because blue has 12, green has 1 and red has 10. I added and I got 23. Then I counted the students in the class and it was the same number.

In order to get to this point, there was a lot of discussion among themselves. This activity took me about 2 hours. The next day they combined both graphs in one and then wrote statements about the graphs.

These are some of the statements my students wrote about comparing both graphs:

1. I can see that in both graphs the fourth and fifth graders like blue more than the other colors, because the fifth grade got 12 in the blue and the fourth graders got 7 on the blue.
2. In the fifth grade there are more people that like blue than the fourth grade.

3. Yo veo que solo a una persona del cuarto año le gusta el amarillo. En el quinto año a nadie le gusta el amarillo.

4. The green in the fourth grade has more than in the fifth grade.

The activity went OK with my class. It seems they have a harder time making comparisons between the graphs and reading the graphs when they are together. They did much better when the graphs were presented individually.

Dear Carlos,

Your class did a very complete job of answering this question. They came up with their own question, so they understood what the data are and what they are comparing. I liked very much the instruction to write three statements about the graph. This pushed them to describe the data (and to say more than one thing about the data). They also had to design their representation.

I think it was very important that you asked them to show both sets of data. I agree with you that learning how to use graphs to show comparisons is challenging. Now that they have tried this, could they benefit from having some discussion about which representations are easiest to use to see the comparison between the two grades? This might help all of them learn to make comparisons. Some students, for example Maria, have carefully placed one graph above the other, but the colors for the fifth grade are in a different order than the colors for the fourth grade. This could make the two graphs more difficult to compare. Some students have made good efforts to show the two groups together (Marisela, Karen). For example, Karen puts the two graphs directly over each other, with the same colors lined up. Do you think students could start discussing how best to make a graph show a comparison?

I have one more suggestion. Now that your students have some experience with categorical data, I think they should have some experience with numerical data. Maybe some of the cases will give you some ideas about data they could collect—number of people in their families, or number of brothers and sisters, or number of countries or states where they've lived, etc. I am hoping you will be able to do some more work with data as the year goes on.

Maxine

Karen had her second graders count pockets and compare the number in their own class with the number in another class. She had felt rushed and somewhat dissatisfied with what she had done. Still, she had made a good start with her students in comparing data, and I wanted to point out how she might build on this experience.

Karen
November 10

It was very hard for me to find a time when we could actually get data from another class because it was quite busy with our class play and the Book Fair going on at our school.

Today, I quickly got the data from another class and charted it on the board. I put the charts side-by-side so the children could compare them.

Pocket Day

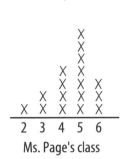

Ms. Page's class

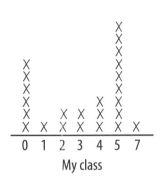

My class

EARNEST:	There are more pockets in our class than in Ms. Page's.
ME:	What do you mean?
EARNEST:	There are more people with 5 pockets in our class.

Was he commenting on the fact that with more 5-pocketed people in our class, we would have more pockets overall?

TYRONE:	There are two people with 3 pockets in our room and in Ms. Page's room.
LESLIE:	No one in our class has 6 pockets!
CARIANA:	Yeah, but no one in Ms. Page's class has 7 pockets like me!

The children agreed that 5 pockets seemed to be quite popular today.

ME:	Will the chart look different tomorrow?
LESLIE:	Yes, because tomorrow we have gym and most of us will be wearing sweats!
ME:	Well, what if you didn't have gym tomorrow? Would the chart stay the same?
EARNEST:	I think that it might basically remain the same.
ME:	Why?

This sparked a little debate among the children.

TYRONE:	Tomorrow I might wear more pockets.
BROOKE:	I'll be wearing my sweats, so, um, I'll have no pockets still!

I asked them to comment on the fact that we had so many people with no pockets. I had the people with no pockets stand up. Of the 6 people, 5 of them were girls. I was hoping they'd comment on the fact that most of the people in this group were girls. They observed that the girls in the group were wearing white. So I asked them what the chart would look like if I took data from a classroom full of only girls.

CHRIS: I think that there'd be a lot of people with no pockets.

ME: Why?

KIMMY: Only when we wear these kinds of dresses.

ME: It looks as if it is time to go home, but we'll try something like this again soon. You all had some very interesting things to say!

I wish I had done this homework activity earlier. I had hoped to be able to ask more questions or probe further, but our time was limited. The children were very engaged and interested and had lots more to say and I was generally pleased with their observations.

Dear Karen,

Even though you weren't satisfied, it seems to me this activity provided a reasonable start for your students in comparing two groups. They were certainly noticing some important things: there were a lot of people with 5 pockets in both classrooms; only your class had someone with 7 pockets. I was wondering when Earnest said "there are more pockets in our class," if he was noticing that there are more people represented on your graph than on the graph for Ms. Page's class. It just kind of jumps out at you that there are more X's on your graph. But then when he talked about the people with 5 pockets, I wasn't sure either if he was comparing only the tallest columns on each graph or whether he was relating that to the total number on each graph.

For next time, here are some things I was wondering. It was interesting that they didn't seem to notice that there were a lot of people with 0 pockets in your class and none at all in Ms. Page's class. Do students think the zeroes don't matter? Would they have noticed this if you had spent more time describing each graph carefully before comparing them? Would they have noticed something about zero if zero had been shown on the other graph also? That brings me to another set of questions for you and your students: Is there a reason to show the numbers that have no data (for example, 6 for your class and 0 and 1 for Ms. Page's class)? How would this change their view of what the data show?

Even though this activity was quick, I think you've started something you can build on.

Maxine

Maxine's Journal

November 18

I knew that many participants had brought up the mean—an average that was familiar to them—earlier in the course. I was looking forward to this opportunity to delve into the structure and use of the mean and to continue our discussions about average. At the same time, I knew I had to leave a good half of this session for a discussion of casebook chapter 8, "Highlights of Related Research."

Math activity: Working with the mean

As I watched the teachers share their homework, I noticed several ways in which participants had created lists of prices for the five bags of potato chips. Some people had made $1.38 the median by simply choosing two prices higher than $1.38 and two prices lower than $1.38. In one group, there was some lively discussion about how $1.38 would still be the median no matter how much bigger and smaller the other prices were. Another solution was to find prices that "balanced" around $1.38, so that for each price above $1.38, there was also a price the same amount below $1.38; an example of a list like this was Regina's: $1.30, $1.36, $1.38, $1.40, $1.46.

In developing lists of prices that did *not* include $1.38, some participants tried to use the median or mean. One group decided that, if you thought of the average as a median, there was no way to do this with an odd number of pieces of data—the middle value would have to be $1.38. Quite a few participants had worked backward from their knowledge of the formula for finding the mean to a realization that the sum of the five prices had to be 5 x $1.38. They then used that total, $6.90, and created prices by subtracting each price from the total. Judith had a list of prices, developed through this method, as follows: $1.30, $1.35, $1.37, $1.39, and $1.49. The group was looking at this list and wondering how to "see" that $1.38 was the average.

Marilyn said, "I know I can figure out that it's $1.38 by adding up all the numbers and dividing by 5, but I want it to make sense. There ought to be a way that it makes sense by looking at it."

Paul observed, "Well, there are three prices below and only two above, but the $1.49 is further away. Even though there are only two different prices, the $1.49 kind of pulls the average up." This group was beginning to focus on something important about the "weight" of the values—how the distances between these values and the mean balance.

Several participants had not found any way to create a list of prices with an average of exactly $1.38 without using $1.38 itself. Donald was describing his thinking to his group. He had first created two lists of prices: (a) $1.35, $1.36, $1.37, $1.39, $1.40, and (b) $1.36, $1.37, $1.39, $1.40, $1.41. He explained that at first he thought these were as close as you could get to $1.38 without using $1.38. He had calculated the mean of the first list as $1.374 and the mean of the second list as $1.386. He kept thinking about how to get closer and explained to his group that he realized he could duplicate values, so he tried $1.37, $1.37, $1.37, $1.39, and $1.39. He calculated a mean of $1.378, which rounds to $1.38, and felt sure that he was as close as possible. Others in his group seemed quite impressed with his strategy.

I asked, "So there's no way you could have a group of five bags of potato chips with a mean of *exactly* $1.38?"

Barbara said, "There ought to be some way, but I don't see how. When you actually do it, you can't get any closer." I suggested they go on to work on question 2, while keeping this question in mind.

For question 2, groups easily made representations of the five bags of peanuts with cubes. Most groups also easily created a line plot with these data.

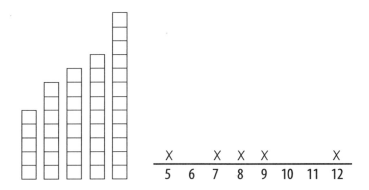

One group was confused at first—did I really mean for them to make a line plot with just five pieces of data? It was so sparse, I think it looked strange to them. Suzanne said, "There's no shape to it—it's just flat." I acknowledged that we wouldn't usually bother making a graph for such a small data set, but that in this case, the representations were tools to help us explore how the mean represents the data set.

At least two of the groups noticed that the cube representation they had made was a case value plot whereas the line plot showed frequency. As Diana put it, "In the line plot, each X is a whole thing." I asked her to elaborate, and she said, "The X for 5 doesn't *look* any different than the X for 7—it's just where it is on the number line that tells you. But with the cubes, the stack of 7 is taller than the stack of 5."

In another group, there was a prolonged argument about whether there could be a bag with 0 peanuts in it. Carlos and Annie maintained that there could, Melissa and Donald that there couldn't. Annie said, "We're thinking about bags, but you're thinking about peanuts."

After listening for a while, I thought that they might not be addressing the same question. Donald and Melissa seemed to be arguing that in a real context, you wouldn't have a bag with no peanuts in it—if it was "a bag of peanuts," it had to have some peanuts. Annie and Carlos seemed to be considering the problem as inviting them to experiment with different combinations of numbers, as a way of learning something about how the mean behaves. For them, the context was just a way of posing the problem. I proposed that there were two different questions: one of context (could you really have a value of 0 in this context?) and a mathematical question (what happens if you *do* have a value of 0?). Donald and Melissa didn't want to budge off their context issue.

I finally decided to be pretty directive. I told them, "My goal today is for you to explore how the mean relates to a set of data. I think it's important to consider what happens when there are values of 0 in the data set. So, if you want to change the context in your head, that's fine—for example, you could say these values are the number of days absent for 7 different students. But I think you should move on now to continue your work on the rest of question 2."

By this time, most groups had found values for the two extra bags, had added these to their representations, and were trying to "see" where the average was in their representation. Ellen's group was working on a representation that showed how the average was an "evening out" of the data. They started with 7 stacks of cubes, one for each piece of data, with a different color for each stack. They used the colors of the cubes to keep track of which cubes had been moved to even out the heights of the stacks. You could see where the four white cubes had been moved from the white stack, for example. Many groups had done a similar kind of evening out, but this group's use of color made for a particularly informative representation.

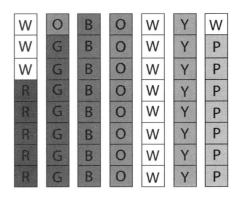

Whole-group discussion As we gathered as a whole group, I decided to have Ellen's group share their colored-cube representation first. Their explanation and the colors seemed to help people see how the cubes had been moved and how the average could be interpreted as a "fair share."

When I asked for other representations, Regina offered a line plot that showed a symmetrical distribution, with the values at 4, 5, 7, 8, 9, 11, and 12. The group explained how the differences from the mean could be matched on each side. I drew in arrows with the differences marked.

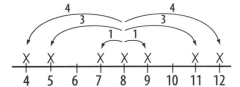

There were several "ahas!" in response to this explanation. I paused to let this idea sink in and to see what questions or confusions might be expressed about it.

Marilyn said that their group had used 2 and 13 as the additional two values, and that these had worked out in their cube model, but that when they added them to their line plot, "it doesn't balance." I put their line plot on the board.

I asked if anyone in the group could show how these values balance. Everyone looked stumped. Rosa, who had also been in Marilyn's group said, "We know it does come out—if you add them up and divide, it's 8—but we don't see why." I could see that there was very little idea about how a balance around the mean worked when the values weren't all balanced pairs (i.e., one value 2 above the mean balanced by one value 2 below the mean, etc.). I suggested that we look at a set of 4 bags in which one bag was 8 and the mean is 8. By choosing an even number of bags in which one bag was equal to the mean, I was forcing the issue of creating an average of 8 with 3 bags.

Judith suggested we try two bags of 7, one of 8, and one of 10. She couldn't explain why this worked—"it just seems like it would be right."

Larry said, "It works if you add them and divide."

Karen said, "If you did it with cubes, you would take 2 off the 10, and put one on each of the 7's, and it would balance."

I drew a line plot of these data and asked, "So where's the balance?"

There was a long wait, and I was wondering what I would do if no one could make sense of the mean using this representation. Finally, Rosa raised her hand tentatively and said, "I think I see it. It's like Karen said about the cubes—the 10 is two away from the 8, and each of the 7's is one away from the 8, so they balance." I drew arrows indicating what she had said so that our representation looked like this:

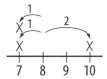

Larry added, "if you call the differences –1, –1, and +2, they add to 0." Then we went back to Marilyn's example, and together worked out how to show how the values balanced around the mean.

Donald was practically jumping up and down in his chair. "Now I see how I could have solved the potato chip problem without the $1.38!"

I wish there had been time to send everyone back into small groups to work on another similar problem. I had the feeling that many participants were just on the edge of grasping how the mean is related mathematically to the data, but needed more experience. I knew there were many more questions to pursue, for example, about how the mean is affected by extreme values. I planned to encourage everyone to finish the Averages, Part 2 sheet for homework but, realistically, I knew that they would be working hard on their final projects and that those projects and the last set of cases would take priority.

I was also somewhat concerned that in plunging so deeply into the mathematics of the mean, participants might have lost sight of what it is that the mean tells you about the data. However, I knew we'd have a chance to return to this issue when we discussed the cases in our last session. We probably needed some time to let these ideas settle.

I closed the discussion by mentioning that it had once been commonplace to teach students how to calculate the mean as early as fourth grade. While students can certainly learn the procedure as soon as they know how to add and divide, our own work with the mean is beginning to reveal some of the complexities of understanding this mathematical object and how it represents the data. I pointed out that in the NCTM's *Principles and Standards for School Mathematics* (2000), the median is suggested for grades 3–5, while the mean is emphasized in grades 6–8. I asked the teachers to keep this in mind as they read the cases in chapter 7.

Highlights of related research

I know from other DMI seminars that reading the research essay can be both challenging and fascinating for teachers. I was eager to see what reading the essay had been like for my group and whether they found the information in it to be useful or intriguing or surprising.

With 20 participants, I didn't have enough people to assign groups of three to each theme in the essay. Besides, the sections in the essay vary in complexity and length, so it made sense to combine some of the shorter ones. I divided participants into five groups of four and assigned the sections as follows:

Group 1: Sections 1 and 2
Group 2: Section 3
Group 3: Sections 4 and 5
Group 4: Section 6
Group 5: Sections 7 and 8

Participants got to work in small groups. They seemed to take seriously their responsibility to explain and illustrate each theme. In the first group, discussing sections 1 and 2, Rosa was saying that she had never considered, before this course, that creating the question was a significant part of the whole process of collecting and analyzing data.

Donald agreed. "I would just throw a question out there—you know, what's your favorite flavor ice cream or something. It never occurred to me that the question mattered."

Carolyn laughed and said, "Well, we sure found out in our project that it mattered! We've been through about 10 different versions of our question."

There was a pause, then Rosa said, "So how are kids going to learn this? If we're always giving them questions, they're not going to learn it. They have to go through trying out something that doesn't work and suffer the consequences. We can't be editing their questions for them. They have to muck around like we did for our projects and figure out that their question doesn't work."

I was interested in what Rosa had to say because earlier in the seminar, when we'd read Beverly's first case ("Do You Like to Eat Soup?"), quite a few people—including Carolyn—had criticized Beverly for unduly limiting the students by providing *yes* and *no* as the options for responses. I wondered what the group saw as the teacher's role in this process. Did they mean that the teacher *never* provides questions? What does the teacher do to help students learn about developing their own questions (or categories)? I asked the group what they thought about the teacher's role.

Nancy, who was often pretty quiet, said, "Well, I know you couldn't throw my special needs kids into this without some experience. I think they'd need a lot of help. You'd have to spend time talking about whether their question worked."

Rosa added, "I think that sometimes you just want to collect data and analyze it and not spend forever going back and forth about what the question is. But sometimes you'd want to really focus on this idea—you'd have to try something out, then have a debriefing to help students decide if they got the data they wanted to get."

The next group was deep into discussion of section 3, "Creating and Interpreting Data Displays," arguing whether one kind of representation can be considered "better" than another. Barbara was saying, rather adamantly, that if a graph serves the purpose for which it was intended, if it shows the data clearly, then you can't say some other graph is better—it might just be a different way of representing it. She noted the sentence in the essay, "decisions about how big to make a graph, whether to label axes or provide titles, should depend on our purposes and should not be made according to a fixed list of 'graph dos and don'ts.'"

Suzanne, who apparently had been articulating a different point of view before I came over, said, "I'm just saying that as you get older, you ought to get more sophisticated. I don't want my third graders to be doing pictographs—it takes too much time, and they should be learning more efficient ways."

Marilyn said, "But pictographs are important for my kindergartners. Isn't this a pictograph?" She pointed to Figure 45 in the essay. "And it's really just like a bar graph anyway."

Sheila, who had been silent up until then, said, "What does it mean for a graph to be more 'abstract'? I don't think I really get this." They began looking at that part of their section, and I moved on.

I was curious to see how the group discussing section 6, "Summarizing Data with Averages," was doing. I expected this section to be difficult because it is lengthy, cites quite a bit of research, and introduces some unfamiliar ways of characterizing interpretations of average. But the group was very organized. They were making a list of what they had learned from this section. So far, they had the following statements:

1. Very young students rely on the mode almost exclusively as a descriptor.
2. Ideas are based on qualitative, rather than quantitative, notions of typicality.
3. Students latch onto the mode rather than average. (Allowance)
4. Students latch on to what "feels" right. (Suzanne's case)
5. Clumps may supersede mode if there is not a clear "winner."
6. Context and the question determine whether students use median or mode, etc.

7. Average is not a precise location but an around-or-about location. (Suzanne's case)

I wondered about statement 5—whether they were thinking of middle clumps as just a sort of enhanced mode, or whether they saw these as a reasonable way of representing the data. I was also curious about the last statement. Was this their view of average or their description of students' views? I didn't get to ask these questions because they were talking about when to teach the median and mean. Paul said he had always taught mean to his fifth graders, but now he was wondering if they were ready to learn about it at that age. Karen said the essay seemed to be saying that median was pretty difficult to understand, too, and Larry noted that he'd come in feeling sure he knew what mean and median were, but now he thought there was a lot more to them. I was wondering whether they would get to think about the three interpretations of average—average as a data reducer, as a fair share, or as a typical value.

Time was almost up, but I quickly checked in on the group discussing sections 7 and 8. I was glad to see that they were talking about section 8 and were deep in a discussion about the student dialogue quoted in that section. They were noticing that this section was very related to section 1. Carlos said, "It's opposite—first you go from the question to the data, now you have to go from the data back to the question."

Each of the theme-discussion groups now counted off, 1 through 4, and we made four new groups of all the ones, twos, threes, and fours. I asked them to appoint a timekeeper in their group so that they would be sure to get to all eight themes during the next 45 minutes. As the recombined groups worked together, I heard many of the same subjects that had been discussed in the theme groups. I hadn't heard the section 3 group talk about the difference between case value plots and frequency plots, but they apparently had spent some time with this idea because it came up in all the combined groups. Although we had previously talked about this idea in Session 3, participants were still grappling with it. Some of the teachers liked having the terms *case value plot* and *frequency graph* to help them talk about the differences; others found these terms a little intimidating, and several groups needed to talk about what *case value* meant.

Viewing data as an aggregate also emerged as a strong theme that participants thought was discussed in a helpful way in the essay. Ellen said, "This is exactly what I see in kindergarten. They are thinking of each thing on the graph as a person; they're not really stepping back and looking at the whole."

Donald, another kindergarten teacher who happened to be in the same group as Ellen, offered, "But don't they start when they're saying things like, 'Red has the most'?"

In the whole group, Karen asked, "Do you think research will show different things once students have more opportunity to work with data? We know that most students haven't done all that much with data, so the research doesn't show what they might be able to do in the future."

Donald added, "And they even said—didn't they say this?—that there wasn't so much research about a lot of these ideas, and so the cases are really important information, too."

I thought this was a critical point—that Karen and Donald were noticing something important about the relationship between teaching and research. I commented, "So if researchers just look at students the way they are, they may see a snapshot of student understanding at a particular time, but if the researcher is undertaking a teaching experiment, it gives the researcher the chance to see how students' understanding might change?"

Judith responded, "I never really thought of research and teaching being connected. I just thought researchers did something off in their offices that mostly didn't have anything to do with what I have to do every day. I thought it was very . . . you know, disconnected, just theory. But while I was reading this, and after taking this course, I was thinking, well *I'm* interested in how my students think. I could be studying that—it doesn't seem so disconnected."

This seemed a perfect point on which to end our discussion.

Exit-card responses

In these exit cards, I was pleased to see that many participants were visualizing a model of "balance" or "evening out" as they described the mean. For example, Annie wrote:

> The mean is like the fulcrum, the balance point around which the other pieces of data "balance." It tells me about what's typical—even if that specific thing does not exist. It pulls together the highs and the lows into the middle. Seeing how to balance things not only means seeing what the numbers are but their placement, distance away from the mean.

However, quite a few participants are still sorting out what the mean is. Melissa wrote, "I need time to digest it to make it my own." There are also a few who show some real confusion over the mean and median. For example, Sheila asked if the median and mean are always the same. I was surprised that this is still a question for anyone. A couple of teachers seem to be relying only on their knowledge of the algorithm for computing the mean, and I wasn't sure from their comments what the impact of today's work had been.

We could probably spend another two sessions on the mean and what it shows about the data, but of course we don't have that much time. I'll have to decide whether to spend a little time during next session's case discussion helping the teachers clarify some of their questions.

Responding to the Seventh Homework

November 22

I found Ellen's essay very interesting, particularly her internal dialogue with the writer of one of the cases. After commenting on Georgia's case in chapter 5, she wrote the following:

> . . . My other strong reaction came from Evelyn's case about mittens. The first set of responses from her students ("we should wear hats and mittens when it's cold," etc.) looked just like what kindergartners say. I reacted pretty strongly, though, to the fact that she made the graph up completely on her own. The students didn't seem to know that when she individually asked them what their favorite color mitten was, it was going to be looked at later. However, when the students were going to poll the first grade, they had many more responses related to the data that was showing (rather than what they knew about mittens). I felt like Homer Simpson—Doh! Of course the students are going to have more to say about what they see because they actually had something to do with it! They were invested in it. Because they had some of the background, they were then able to talk more about the data from their own graph. After this, I thought, "Why would I ever do a data investigation with my children without having their involvement in the design and collection?" I was feeling pretty smug and like I really needed to call Evelyn and say, "What were you thinking?" when I realized that sometimes people need to be able to interpret data that they had no involvement with. Then I felt like calling Evelyn to apologize. Maybe it's really important to see what children do with a visual representation of data with no previous involvement. Children probably need a lot of experience with both. Now I just feel like calling Evelyn to talk about data investigation in kindergarten.

Ellen's reflection on her own critique of Evelyn really captured what it means to learn about teaching by focusing on children's thinking. I thought it might be worthwhile to read this part of her paper to the group. As the seminar has progressed, participants have become more and more skilled at analyzing student thinking, but there is a lingering tendency to "fix" the teaching in the cases—a sense that "if only" the teacher had done something differently, the students would understand more clearly. I thought that everyone would relate to Ellen's dialogue with Evelyn and that its humor would make the point better than I ever could. Ellen seems to be very open to

Working with Data

learning by observing her students' work, but in my response, I also wanted to urge her to begin to articulate some specific learning goals for her students. After commenting on her writing about Georgia's case, I went on to say:

> I love your "dialogue" with Evelyn! I agree with you that there are many aspects to working with data. Often, as adults, we are in the position of trying to interpret data with which we had no direct involvement. However, we can call on our own experience in working with data to help us look critically at data collected by someone else. My guess is that Evelyn, like lots of us, was learning as she went along. Perhaps she would now begin differently. The important thing to me is that she used her students' work as data to inform her own teaching and developed a hypothesis about what a good next step might be, just as you will probably be doing. I think your idea of having conversations with the authors of these cases is a really helpful one. Would you mind if I read part of your episode aloud in class?

Sheila had not done her classroom case for Session 6, but handed it in along with her assignment for this session. Throughout the course, Sheila has seemed to fluctuate between rejecting most of what we are doing in the course as not being relevant to her young special needs students and finding some of the ideas useful to her own teaching. These two assignments showed some of that contrast.

Sheila
November 20

Sixth homework: Students' Thinking about Comparing Groups

> This activity was impossible to do with my students. The concept of comparing two things at this point in the year was excruciatingly painful for both them and me. I started off with the question, "What is the difference between September and October's weather? What do you notice about the weather?" I got answers that ranged from when their birthdays are to the lunch is good today. Then we made big graphs. We also used interlocking cubes so they can see the sunny days versus the cloudy days, etc. I thought they had a clearer concept of the representation, but alas they don't.

> Your next question is, Didn't you try something easier? Well, yes I did. And again that was painful. They are not there. I feel it is too abstract for them to grasp.

Seventh homework: Reflecting on the Cases

> The "Favorite Colors: Where Is the Math?" case struck a familiar cord with me while I was reading. Every year I do a unit on colors. The issue of favorite colors always comes up. Five-year-olds are at a stage where the world is about *them*. I usually set the colors for them on the

graph. But after reading this case study and analyzing data, I chose to do the activity differently. I let the class generate a list of colors that they thought we should graph as our favorites. I found that they had more of an interest because they had an investment in the activity. It was not totally teacher directed. There was much more participation, and language was being used more extensively. I was pleased with the results of this lesson. Although there was not a lot of math talk going on, the students demonstrated that they were capable, motivated, and invested. This made me take a step back and realize that keeping the conversation structured will not give the best results.

The "Today's Question" case actually cleared up some, if not all, of my frustration in dealing with this lesson in my own class. I liked how the teacher had a survey helper. I was becoming frustrated because even though the question was read to all the students, the data were usually misleading. I start with yes-or-no questions. Due to the population of my class, students tend to forget the question. I basically stole the teacher's idea of having a helper. This little change made a difference in the survey results. The students did not appear to be copying their peers' answers. They now had one-on-one help from a peer! Self-esteem was rising, and again the class was excited about the question because they all know at some point they will be helping the teacher. The students have learned one-to-one correspondence, students' names (from the clothespins), and recognize words, numbers, and a multitude of other things. I thoroughly look forward to this activity because it can generate a number of questions that will lead to another data activity.

I was disappointed that Sheila had not felt that she could modify the first assignment in a way that made sense for her students. I try to establish an atmosphere in the course in which participants understand that they should use the course ideas and assignments in a way that helps them think about teaching and learning. I wondered if blaming the assignment was a way for Sheila to send me a message about how the course was inadequate in meeting her needs and the needs of her students. On the other hand, I was glad that she had written honestly to me about the difficulties she had faced. In addition, her writing about the cases offered glimmers of some insight into her own teaching and some willingness to reflect on how her teaching choices impact her students' opportunities to learn. In my response, I wanted to communicate my respect for the challenges of her student population and encourage her to continue to push her own thinking.

Dear Sheila,

Thank you for writing to me about what was troublesome about the assignment, what you tried, and why it was so difficult. You know your students and what is possible. I completely respect that you tried and decided that these activities are not educationally valuable for them at this time.

You seemed to have some success when you first did the data activity for the homework for our second session. What characteristics of that activity made it work? Is there a way that you could select some additional experiences like that in order to continue with data work in a way that is meaningful for your students? I was thinking about the videotape of the grade 2 group collecting pocket data. You certainly wouldn't do it in exactly the same way that class did, but you might be able to make appropriate modifications. For example, I've seen younger students count their pockets by actually putting a cube in every pocket, then taking out the cubes, making a tower, and counting how many cubes they have. Would something like this context, in which they can directly connect the representation (the cubes) to what it is representing (the pockets), be accessible to them?

From your description of the two cases that had an impact on you, it sounds as if you are figuring out some important things about working with data with your students and that you have made good use of the cases in finding ideas that you can apply in your teaching. I am always amazed that so often something small, a small variation on an activity—in your case, the "survey helper"—can make such a difference in how students respond to it. As a special education teacher, you surely are always thinking, What can I do to give my students access to this activity or to this idea? How can I modify it so that they can participate in it meaningfully?

One last comment: I was struck by your statement that "keeping the conversation structured will not give the best results." So often I hear special education teachers say the opposite—that they must structure everything tightly. Certainly, many kinds of structures are important (or none of us would survive in a classroom!), but you seem to be sorting out *which* structures are helpful (like the survey helper) and which structures act to disconnect the students from the activity. Over time, I bet you will see more math talk, as students get more used to this kind of discussion.

Maxine

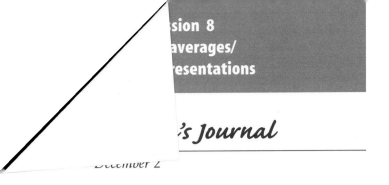

's Journal

December 2

Students arrived for the last class with quite a bustle of excitement. Groups were carrying posters of their project work and were finalizing details for their presentations. I could tell that most participants' minds were completely on their presentation, so I decided to have them set up their posters or other display as they came in, rather than putting this off until break. This would give us a late start, but we could save some time later if they used the break to walk around and look at the projects.

Video preview: Discussing the data

After the projects were set up, I gathered everyone and told them the schedule for the day. I assured them that we'd have a good amount of time to spend on the projects, but that we were first going to spend an hour on a video and our last case discussion. I pointed out the stem-and-leaf plot I had posted, showing the height data from the video they were about to see, and I asked them to spend a few minutes talking to a neighbor about how they would answer the question, *Which class is taller?*

I gave them only about 3 minutes to talk in pairs. I wanted to keep to the planned schedule so the project presentations wouldn't be shortchanged. Then I asked pairs to share their ideas. Donald observed that more than half the first graders are as tall as fourth graders. When I asked him to explain further, he clarified, "Well, there are some fourth graders that are the same height—from 50 inches to 54 inches. They overlap."

Melissa added, "We noticed the overlap, too, but the percentages are different. Only a few fourth graders are from 50 to 54 inches, but a lot of first graders are."

Regina and Suzanne had also thought about percentages. Regina explained, "We noticed that 16 out of 21 of the fourth graders are taller than any first grader, so that's about 75 percent of the fourth graders." Quite a few other participants offered observations, using percentages of the data to compare the groups.

I was pleased that some teachers were looking at chunks of the data and thinking about percentages as a way to describe the data, but I also wanted them to think about the averages we'd been studying and whether these averages could help them describe the differences between the two groups. I knew from the exit cards that many participants were still coming to grips with the mean and median. Since time was short, I decided to ask directly whether anyone had used the median or mean and how those statistics might help compare groups.

Ellen said, "We found the median, and the median of the first grade is 5 inches shorter than the median for the fourth grade." I asked Ellen to tell me the two medians—51.5 inches for first grade, 57 inches for fourth grade—and I wrote them on the chart next to the graph of the data. (If no one had already done this, I would have asked the group to figure out both the mean and the median.)

Judith had been working with her calculator while we talked and reported the means as 50.8 for grade 1 and 56.7 for grade 4. I wrote these down as well, and also asked a couple of people to double-check that we had the right values for the medians and means while we continued to talk.

I didn't want to spend much longer on this discussion, but I hadn't yet heard anyone talk about how the medians or means would help compare the two groups, so I decided to ask one more question before showing the videotape. "I've written down the median heights and the mean heights. At the beginning of this discussion, a lot of you were talking about clumps and percentages in order to compare the two groups. How could either the mean or the median help us answer the question, Which class is taller?"

Carolyn said, "I'd rather use percentages. I don't like using just one number. When you pick just one number, it can really be misleading."

It was quiet for a minute. Carolyn had said this in such a definitive tone that I was afraid it was going to stop the conversation. But then Rosa said slowly, "I know what you mean. It's like we've said before—there's a lot you don't know. But I think if someone told me the medians were 51 inches and 57 inches, I'd have this sense that the fourth graders were shifted over—that they were quite a bit taller."

Larry added, cryptically, "Or the means."

And Marilyn said, "Even the means—I'm sort of thinking of using the cubes. If you evened out all those heights and got 57, you have a lot more inches than if you evened them out and got 51."

Then Suzanne raised a new point. "In this case, the mean and the median are really close together—they're both around 51 inches for first and 57 inches for fourth. But what if they weren't? How would you choose which one to use?"

Suzanne's question was really a good one, but I felt that we just weren't going to have time to do justice to it. Underlying her question was another question: What would a data set look like in which the median and mean were quite different? Always there are some questions left open when a seminar ends, and this was a good time to mention this. I said, "Suzanne's question raises some very interesting problems. What do data sets look like in which the median and mean are close together? What would a data set look like if the median and mean were not close together? This would be a great question for you to continue to explore. It's not going to be possible to bring closure to all the ideas that have come up in this seminar, just as it's not possible in the classroom. We've had to choose some for our focus, and I'm hoping that you'll go further with these ideas on your own. But at this point I'd like to show the video and move into our case discussion."

Video viewing and small-group discussion

I had everyone take notes on the video; then they moved to small groups for the case discussion. I wanted them to get to at least the first two questions, and if possible the third, so I kept track of the time and periodically suggested that groups move on to the next question.

Most groups were able to list the different features or measures students used to compare data sets: the most common, the middle, the extremes, clumps, the total of all the values (an idea in Maura's case 27 that also seems to be foundational to understanding the mean).

As one group talked about question 2, Larry stated that Trudy (in Phoebe's case 26, line 137) "really gets the mean," but Suzanne gently challenged him: "I'm not so sure. She does know how to add up and divide, but does she have any idea why she's doing that?" The group went on to have a productive discussion about how they would know if a student "really got" the mean.

At one point, Rosa asked, "What does it mean for *us* to really get the mean? Do we?"

Later, when I came around again, I heard Larry reflecting, "You know, my class always has an issue when there are 14 kids on one team and 12 on the other, and they're finding the mean—they think it's not fair. They don't get that finding the mean is what makes it fair—it eliminates the difference in team size." This remark started another round of discussion. Rosa and Helen weren't so sure they understood how the mean "eliminated" differences in size.

Several groups talked quite a bit about Gabe (also in Phoebe's case 26, line 193). Participants noticed that he had a beginning idea of values balancing around the mean, but as the conversation continued, it seemed that his idea might be more about finding a middle value—Karen said that she thought his thinking was based more on "in-betweenness" than on the idea of balancing. Nancy was impressed that he could think of an average as a number that wasn't a value in the data set, but that it still somehow represented those data.

Working with Data

Groups were having good discussions, so I decided to bring them back together for only 5 minutes before break. Rather than looking specifically at any of the questions, I asked them what they had noticed about students' developing ideas about average in the video and the cases.

Barbara said, "There are so many ways to think about average—the kids switch back and forth between them. As teachers, we switch back and forth between them as well."

Paul commented, "We don't have really good language to deal with common, typical, average. Do all these words mean the same thing? What do students think we mean when we use them? What do *we* think we mean?"

Regina noted that in some of the examples "there seems to be rote learning of an algorithm, but there doesn't seem to be much meaning attached to it." There were murmurs of assent, and then Larry and Rosa talked a little about their group's discussion about how we would know whether or not students understand median or mean.

I brought the discussion to a close—feeling that we were still in the middle of so much—and gave instructions that we would spend the next 20 minutes taking a quick break and looking at each other's projects.

Project presentations

As I looked over the projects myself and listened to the small-group interactions, I was quite fascinated with the variety of decisions that had been made about presentation and analysis. Some groups chose to talk about mean, median, and mode, but not all. Some reported on those, but didn't really draw conclusions from them. Some did stem-and-leaf or box plots, but not all. Some seemed to really connect with the data and analyze it in a way that made sense for that data, while others just reported what they saw without really thinking critically about it. However, all of them were much advanced over their pilot study. They have learned so much, especially about formulating the questions and evaluating their data in light of the purpose of their study.

Many of the other ideas of the seminar were touched on: developing representations, summarizing data, comparing groups, and using statistical measures such as averages. The members of one group talked about how they had been trying to figure out the mean and kept getting numbers that they knew weren't right. Finally they realized they had been adding up the number of people at each value instead of the values they represented. They said they will never forget this learning experience as an example of knowing the procedure but not being able to connect it to meaning until they really thought hard about it together.

Several of the projects had gathered data that was useful to them in thinking about an issue at their school. Sheila, Carolyn, Nancy, and Regina, who had compared the amount of reading at home in grades 1 and 5, had been astonished to find that the grade 5 students were not reading any more than the grade 1 students. These four teachers were very well prepared, had a lot to say, and were eager to share. This was, perhaps, the most connected and involved Sheila has been.

Others had collected data on straightforward topics that were not connected to an issue of concern, but they were nevertheless eager to share their project and had a lot to say about what they had learned about working with data. For example, Diana, Karen, and Annie had asked children, teenagers, and adults, "What temperature makes you feel spring is here?" and Judith and Melissa investigated, "Can first graders jump higher than kindergarten students?" One or two expressed some regret that they hadn't done something "more important," and I reiterated that the purpose of the project was to practice and hone their skills with data, and that what they had learned would be useful for them both in interpreting data and, if the occasion arose, in doing their own data investigations about topics of interest to them.

In general, I noticed that the group process of working on the data projects was very supportive for some people who had really struggled with the math ideas. I can't think of anyone in the group who wasn't a full and focused participant in this part of the session. After the small-group discussions, we had a brief whole-group discussion about what they had learned from their projects and the course in general. They said the project helped them integrate their ideas and see what it is like to try to apply new learning. They felt they had learned a lot about representing data, what it takes to do a good study, and what kinds of questions need to be asked about a study's results. They also said that they've come to see how complex many of these ideas are, and that students need time and experience to develop them.

As we closed our final class, I knew there were still mathematical ideas that everyone had not worked through and that some felt the class had not met all their needs, but in general I felt satisfied that many of the teachers were taking away a richer, more complex notion of the elements of data representation and analysis and a deeper interest in how these tools can be used—by themselves and by their students—to understand the world. As I said goodbye and handed out the portfolio review assignment, I found myself curious and eager to read what they had to say about the course.

Final Reflections

December 18

I spent last night reading through the portfolio reviews that the teachers had mailed to me and writing brief notes to each participant commenting on their portfolio reviews, their data projects, and their participation in the course.

A number of common threads struck me as I read the reviews. First, although many had struggled at various points in formulating or carrying out their data project, it was clear that the project had been a key experience for most participants. For example, Barbara wrote:

> One of the important things I learned by working on our asthma study project is that you always have to remember why you are collecting the data. What ideas will it support? I found it easy to get sidetracked by the different kinds of data we collected and the many different ways it could be represented.

Others, like Helen, commented on how working on the project influenced their work with their students:

> If I had not had to struggle simultaneously with my students, I might have been tempted to think that my students were just not "getting it." Now I know that these struggles are universal no matter how old you are.

It seems clear that carrying out a project from beginning to end— using all the data tools and ideas in order to actually address a particular question— was key to the teachers' experience. Otherwise, the seminar might have been too fragmentary—a series of different ideas and techniques—or too distant— reading about *others* carrying out data investigations. Although I certainly don't want teachers to end up feeling that work with data always has to be a big project that takes many days of class time, I also want them to get the feel of the process of data analysis from beginning to end. I hope that they can use this understanding to balance quick excursions with data—such as we saw on the pocket data video in Session 1—and longer investigations focused on questions of interest and import to the students.

It's also clear that many of the teachers have reevaluated what they once thought was adequate work with data in their classrooms. I was pleased at the clarity with which many of them talked about specific changes in their own practice. Ellen wrote:

> I have already changed my questioning as a result of taking this course. Before the course, I thought my students "got it" if they described data collected with comparative comments ("*yes* got 4 more than *no*"). When I began to ask, "So what does that tell you about our class?" I realized that many students did not relate the data they were describing to the question we had asked.

Rosa described her own thinking and the changes she was already seeing in her third graders:

Ignorance is bliss or ignorance is dangerous. I thought the data activities I typically did with my students were sufficient for them to achieve the standards of learning. I focused my teaching on my students' ability to answer the kinds of questions that are on the standardized tests—usually just reading some information off the graph—rather than on their understanding of the process of working with data. Comparison of data sets seems to really engage my students. The students' descriptions of data changed from basic counting and simple statements to comparing data sets as "more than" or "less than," and explaining how many more or less, and relating this back to the question we asked. I'm very pleased with the change in depth of analysis that has occurred so quickly.

Many teachers wrote specifically about how they will draw on what they learned from the cases in their own classrooms and about how they are now helping their students focus on "the big picture" of the data.

Several participants had come into the seminar with considerable doubt that it would meet their needs. Sheila's response was more upbeat than I expected, given her doubts throughout the course and the first sentence of her review. She wrote:

I came into this course math phobic and I left the course feeling the same way. I realize that I am not a mathematical thinker and find it very difficult to talk math. But yes, I thoroughly enjoy teaching math to my little ones. Go figure.

The data project was extremely interesting for me. Our literacy idea was fantastic in that it is giving us valuable information which we can actually use in our school. I feel that the project brought forth a multitude of questions about where we are going with literacy. I am eager to continue data collection to see if there is any improvement in our scores, in student attitudes, and in parent awareness of the importance of reading at home.

I learned as a special needs teacher that not every second of the day needs to be so structured. I found it amazing to listen to some of the explanations my students came up with (though some were completely off the wall). They enjoy coming up with questions for data collection, and I feel confident that they can be successful with data. I have definitely changed some of my styles in ways that are subtle but enough for me to see the difference in students' work and responses.

In my note to her, I emphasized how much she had learned and that she was clearly thinking hard about how to apply this to her classroom. I questioned whether in fact she was "math phobic" or whether she was just experiencing the same confusions and frustrations that we all encounter with unfamiliar material. I wrote:

> It certainly may be true that there were some others in the group who seemed to 'get' some of the ideas more quickly, but it seems to me that you truly engaged in the mathematics yourself and that you worked through some important ideas, especially while doing your data project. After this experience, I wonder how it would feel now to do some other professional development in mathematics?

I was of course very interested in reading about what participants had to say as they reflected on their own mathematics learning. I was not surprised that a lot of the comments had to do with learning about averages and learning about new data representations. Many participants had enjoyed learning that there are a greater variety of ways to represent data than they had realized. Quite a few of the teachers mentioned ongoing questions they had about averages, as in this excerpt from Donald's review:

> I am still struggling with what mean, median, and mode tell us about the data. No, I know what they tell us, but my question is, what is it important to know? I'm happiest when the mean, median, and mode are close together or, better yet, the same! I still want to think more about when each of them is useful.

One of the issues for me in an eight-session course on this material is that we inevitably leave some loose ends. I have wondered about doing this seminar in ten, rather than eight, sessions. It might give us a slightly more relaxed pace and some additional time to think through questions that remain about averages and to touch on ideas about sampling. However, 24 hours of seminar time is already a big commitment for classroom teachers. Perhaps I will get a chance to try this format in the future.

One important idea came through in many of the responses, even though it was not explicitly addressed in the seminar. As people learn a little about data, they sometimes learn just enough to conclude that because statistics are not certain, they are therefore not useful. However, rather than coming to the conclusion that "all statistics lie," several teachers expressed their growing understanding that there are a variety of ways to view data. For example, Judith wrote:

> I learned that when you start with a question you are interested in, you do have your own hypothesis and this definitely influences how you analyze the information. Going into this course I thought that data was so scientific and not subject to what ideas we bring to the analysis.

Suzanne made related comments:

> The "big picture" or "big ideas" are more evident when a data set is explored from several points of view. It helps prevent children from relying too heavily on any one summary, such as mean, median, or mode.

I was struck by how many participants said that in the past they had assumed that teaching about data was straightforward and clear and that they had never before had the opportunity to think hard about teaching about data. Overall, I felt that we had come a long way in our work together.